Continued
Success!

Jill Griffin

PRAISE for
FOLLOW THESE LEADERS

Jill Griffin's book offers bites of wisdom on every page. These gems have been carefully curated from her network of family, friends, business contacts, and (even and some generous strangers) gathered over a three-decade career. *Follow These Leaders* includes career and life advice AND a primer on building customer loyalty. It's a must-read.
—*Gail Page, Corporate Board Member Chembio, NASDAQ: (CEMI), and Chief Business Advisor Dell Medical School, University of Texas at Austin*

In this warm, heartfelt book, Jill Griffin transforms her personal network of luminaries—one she has cultivated over a lifetime—into your personal board of directors, who crystallize their real-world experience into gem after gem of practical wisdom.
—*John Chisholm, CEO, John Chisholm Ventures, and Past President & Chair, Worldwide MIT Alumni Association*

Follow the leader used to be a game—*Follow These Leaders* makes it a contact sport of success!!! Another must-have best seller from Jill Griffin!
—*Jeffrey Hayzlett, Primetime TV & Podcast Host, Speaker, Author, and Part-Time Cowboy*

Follow These Leaders offers nuggets of wisdom thoughtfully andcarefully collected spanning leadership, career and life skills, and even customer loyalty. Collected from Jill Griffin's lifetime of friendships and great mentors, it's a must-read.
—*Sheila Hooda, CEO, Alpha Advisory Partners, Independent Board Director*

MORE PRAISE for
FOLLOW THESE LEADERS

Jill Griffin's new book, *Follow These Leaders,* is filled from cover to cover with timeless wisdom and truth. Follow these wise and practical leaders and they will lead you to your best life and career, no doubt.
—*Mike Mooney, Author of*
Reputation Shift: Lessons from Pit Road to the Boardroom

#1 in non-fiction March 10, 2019
Book People, Austin, TX

FOLLOW ★ THESE ★ LEADERS

FOLLOW ★ THESE ★ LEADERS

Wisdom and Mentorship from the
Voices of Success

Jill Griffin

Published by Jill Griffin Books
www.jillgriffin.net

Copyright ©2019 Jill Griffin

All rights reserved.

No part of this book may be reproduced, stored in a retrieval system, or transmitted by any means, electronic, mechanical, photocopying, recording, or otherwise, without written permission from the publisher.

Design and composition by Alex Head / Draft Lab
Cover design by Justin Esquivel

ISBN 13: 978-0-9969218-6-2

Printed in the United States of America on acid-free paper

First Edition

This book is proudly dedicated to my beloved high school English teacher, Miss Myrtle Kiker. She inspired so many!

She is the reason I can write books, and I've kept every theme I ever wrote for her.

In college classes when I had a B average, my term paper would get me the A.

I'd almost hear Miss Kiker guiding me on writing the "all-important" opening paragraph that would set the tone for the rest of the paper.

She was in great spirits, and sharp as a tack, when I visited her last year.

Blessings to you, Myrtle Kiker.

Myrtle Kiker 1927-2018

TABLE OF CONTENTS

Dedication vii
Acknowledgments xv
How This Book Came to Be xvii
PART ONE - Career Advice 1
   Be Twice as Good 3
   Best List of Work Basics—Ever 6
   Say Yes . . . and Stretch. 8
   You Can Always Change Your Mind 9
   Be Resourceful 12
   A Turning Point 13
   Slow Down 15
   Crowdsource Your Ideas 17
   Start Fresh Tomorrow. 19
   Guess What? It's Up to You 21
   Stretch 22
   Customer Service 101 24
   Get In over Your Head. 25
   Befriend Your Banker 27
   Lead by Example 29

Listen to the Music	30
Be Prepared	32
Show Up	34
Trust Your Gut	36
Make a Plan	37
Follow the Light	39
If You Knew You Could Not Fail	42
Make a Career Change	45
Don't Do It	47
Girls Can Do Anything	49
Family Lessons	52
Do Something	54
Marketing Matters	56
Find a Mentor	57
Hard on the Task, Easy on the People	58
Assume the Best	60
Two Key Words to Never Forget: Collaborate and Listen	62
Be Visible	64
Shrug Off Negativity	66
Write Your Leadership Credo	67
Be Open to New People	70
Be Inclusive	73
Don't Burn Bridges	75
Honor Wisdom	76
Firing and Hiring	78
Meanness Rarely Helps	79

   Find Your Champion. 81
   Be Happy for Another's Success 82
PART TWO - My Customer Loyalty Beginning. . . 85
   Customer Loyalty Playbook. 87
   Building Loyalty in Your Life! 88
   Building Loyalty by Stages Is Strategic 88
   How to Qualify a Suspect 89
   Turning Qualified Prospects into First-Time
   Customers 90
   Turning First-Time Customers into Repeat
   Customers 90
   Turning Repeat Customers into Clients 92
   Turning Clients into Advocates 93
PART THREE - Life Advice 97
   Realize What's Truly Important 99
   Practice Integrity. 101
   Time Management. 104
   More Time Management. 105
   Never Stop Believing 107
   Bring Your Big Heart. 109
   Keep It Simple. 110
   Wait Three Days 112
   Short, Sweet, Powerful. 114
   Try a New Perspective 115
   Look the Part 116
   Practice Insane Courage 118
   You'll Never Go Wrong 119

Own Your Life	120
Cash In on Social Capital	121
Mission Field or Battlefield?	124
Thanks, Dad	126
Honesty and Integrity Are Not for Sale	127
Leaving Home	129
Don't Get Stuck in the Middle	131
Recognize Your Blessings	133
Work Behind the Scenes	134
Managing Highs and Lows	136
Dress for Success	137
Stay One Step Ahead	138
Pay Attention	140
Passion to Serve	141
Don't Undercut Your Value	142
One Simple Rule	145
Treat Everyone Well	146
Be Genuine	147
There Is No "Big C"	149
Watch, Wait, and Listen	150
Where I Hope This Book Takes You	151
More…	153
Are You Ready to Start a Company?	155
Notes	166
About the Author	167
Index	169

Acknowledgments

Since entering the "New Frontier" of self-publishing, my original team has never changed.

They are highly creative, superb talents, who stay on deadline and, above all, bring me back to center when I go astray:

Cover Design & Webmaster: Justin Esquivel

Publicists: Dennis & Susie Welch

Book Producers: Alex Head & Lari Bishop

Interior Book Designer: Alex Head

Editors: Judy Barrett, Linda O'Doughda

Special Advisors: Cheryl Rae and Karen Post

I wish to thank my sister, Marsha Alexander, and her late husband, D.M. Alexander, and their sons, wives, and grandkids for adding lots of fun to my life.

My love, Doug Glasgow.

"Adoptive" Parents, Sarita & Dan Toma.

Childhood Friends, College, Career, and Austin friends.

How This Book Came to Be

★ ★ ★

I'm an advice seeker by nature, and I have a hunch most people are, too. Like me, hadn't they been given at least one valuable piece of advice that stood out as a turning point in their lives? So I reached out to family, friends, colleagues, and total strangers with this question:

What's a great piece of business or life advice you received, who gave it to you, and how has it enhanced your life?

Turns out, the question was a good one. Emails and LinkedIn responses and Facebook posts and phone calls poured in in response. And, I had the privilege of interacting with speakers and attendees at the 2018 KPMG Women's Leadership Summit in Chicago.

Many people could recall in detail the exact place and time they were given the words of wisdom as well as the emotions that arose in their hearts as the advice sank in. One of my favorite examples is from keynote speaker, international sales trainer, and best-selling author Jeffrey Gitomer:

> Forty years ago I was driving with a client who, at the time, was my biggest customer. A mentor and a friend, he was actually more like a father to me. I made an offhand remark based on a recent success of his. "Mel, you are the *luckiest* person I know. Everything you touch or get involved with turns into gold."
>
> He immediately responded, "Jeffrey, hard work makes luck." I sat in silence for the remainder of the ride, and to this day, I have worked my ass off *every day*.

The coach who worked with Betty Liu, Bloomberg Television's *In the Loop* anchor offered up this simple equation: "Opportunity + Preparation = Luck."

That little survey question spawned a series of related questions.

What makes good advice?

The best advice includes a call for action. For example: Save your money and then pay cash for your car. Don't go out and finance a car you can't afford.

What kind of advice is easiest to take?

Advice that rings true as "common sense" is easy to take. Of course, one's definition of common sense matures over time.

What is there in the listener that makes him or her receptive to taking advice?

Good listeners come with an open mind and an open heart. They are eager to grow and are open to advice that helps them do so. As Olympic gold medal figure skater and sports commentator Tara Lipinski puts it, "Whether you're an athlete or a student, [listening to] an adult who believes in you and can give you advice and wisdom that is coming from a place of experience is an incredible asset to help guide you through your young life."

This openness is often a by-product of having taken a different route and meeting with downright disaster. They've dusted themselves off and are ready for a new direction.

How does trust factor into the equation?

Trust is crucial. As she shared with the *Wall Street Journal*, Peggy Johnson, Microsoft's executive vice president of business development, relies on her "gut" when she must make a big decision. She "validates her intuition," though, by talking with her husband, an independent investor, and reaching out to four trustworthy former colleagues and mentors for their learned advice before she fully makes up her mind.

People generally go to the one person they know who has their best interest at heart. This confidence generally comes from being friends a long time and slowly revealing true selves to one another over time. Trust is fragile and builds slowly. It can be lost in one betrayal.

What makes someone take action?

When advice is so compelling, the "taker" can't wait to take action. For example: My close friend Lisa Webb is a trained psychologist. Sometimes her clients are struggling with the loss of a love due to divorce, a recent separation, or the end of a longtime relationship. To help them through the process of letting go, Lisa gives them homework assignments. One such assignment is to make a list of the times the "love" actually made them feel "unsafe" or "unloved."

Then, at the next session, they review the list with Lisa. She says the emotional shift is powerful. The client begins to see why the loss of the love is, in part, a healthy thing.

Why does worthy advice often go in one ear and out the other?

Often the recipient of a particular word of advice is not ready emotionally to take action. If the person listens to the same advice over and over again without doing anything, his or her family members and close friends should take note of this and back off.

The old saying is true: "You can lead a horse to water but you can't make him drink."

Do you find yourself asking, "Why do I need advice anyway?" This runs through our minds especially in the places where we work and live. But heeding the lessons others have learned the hard way does have its benefits. And in the evocative words of English Romantic poet Samuel Taylor Coleridge, "Advice is like snow—the softer it falls, the longer it dwells upon, and the deeper it sinks into the mind."

- Great advice takes years off your learning curve.
- A person who has gone before you, faced similar hurdles, and crossed the finish line

can be of enormous help in advising you on running the same obstacle course.
- You feel "loved." If someone observes you enough to offer a word of wisdom as to how you can improve, that's a good thing. They care, and you're worth the investment of their time and effort.
- An advice giver and an advice taker often form a strong bond, which brings both of them great satisfaction.
- Make it your goal to earn the right to give worthy advice. That way, you can pay it forward by reaching out your hand to help the next person.

Americans have a long history of seeking advice on matters large and small. (After all, even George Washington wrote about manners, as I reported in my book *Women Make Great Leaders*.) The subject of advice so fascinated award-winning producer and writer Jessica Weisberg that she chronicled it in *Asking for a Friend: Three Centuries of Advice on Life, Love, Money, and Other Burning Questions from a Nation Obsessed* (Nation Books, 2018). It's a good read, full of humor and heart, which reveals that people everywhere, in every era, are vulnerable and insecure and hungry for answers. As Weisberg puts it, "The questions [posed by advice seekers] over time really underscored to me that the things that are challenging about being a person and having human relationships have always been challenging."

We all face challenges as we relate to others in the workplace, the community, and the world at large. What follows are the reflections on Career, Customer Loyalty, and Life I have collected from those in my world.

I sincerely hope they will help you live your life fully—with style and business savvy.

PART ONE

Career Advice

★ ★ ★

I knew in the third grade I was destined to be a "career girl." My teacher, Miss Ellen Gaddy, was my first introduction to someone who had a career and was the sole provider for her own needs. Her life choices inspired me.

All the latest research says that doing a job we love and doing it well is good for us on every level. And, a big part of enjoying that work is getting the most out of every day you spend there. Like most things in life, you only get out of your career what you invest into it. Spend the time and effort, and you are likely to excel.

This section is full of sage advice to help you move ahead and achieve just that.

Be Twice as Good

★ ★ ★

If you are lucky enough to be invited to the KPMG Women's Leadership Summit, go! This book is peppered with what I soaked up at that glorious conference. First up, excerpts from my transcription of an interview with Condoleezza Rice.

The second woman and first African-American woman to hold the post of Secretary of State, Rice credits her parents for putting her on a path to greatness by not letting obstacles get in her way.

As a little girl, someone didn't want to sit next to her because of her race; and when she told her dad, Rice said he told her, "You know what, if they don't want to sit next to you just because you're black, that's just fine, as long as they move."

Rice was raised in segregated Birmingham. Her parents' mantra was: "You have to be twice as good." They taught Rice she could do and be anything as long as she earned her way by being twice as good. In other words, she must hyper-prepare to significantly outperform others.

Rice's childhood dream was to become a concert pianist. She attended the University of Denver as a piano major, and her sophomore year, she fiercely prepared for a "professional" recital in Aspen. There, she witnessed piano prodigies and decided if she had stayed on that track, she would be playing the piano in a department store, she joked.

She came back to school desperate to choose a new major. After a few false starts, she wandered into an International Politics course taught by Josef Korbel, a Soviet specialist. The course ultimately triggered Rice's deep interest in international affairs, especially the Soviet Union's military (Korbel, who is Madeleine Albright's father, became her long time mentor). To this day, Rice names Moscow as her favorite city, having spent a lot of time there researching her PhD dissertation.

Rice's stellar insights at a 1985 meeting of arms control experts attracted the attention of Brent Scowcroft, who became her mentor. With the election of George H. W. Bush, Scowcroft returned to the White House as National Security Advisor in 1989, and he asked Rice to become his Soviet expert on the United States National Security Council. Asked how she had the confidence to be the only woman (and a young one at that) in meetings with powerful men all over the world, she answered that she made sure she was more prepared than anyone else in the meeting. This hard work gave her the confidence "to walk in like I owned the place," she said with a laugh.

But preparedness isn't all you need, added Rice, whom the president chose as the 66th U.S. Secretary of State. You also need strong mentors who will advocate for you. For example, President Bush introduced her to Russian President Gorbachev, saying, "This is Condoleezza Rice. She's my Soviet Specialist. She's from Stanford University. She tells me everything I know about the Soviet Union." Rice believes President Bush was sending a strong message, not just to President Gorbachev, but to everyone within earshot that she was his Soviet expert and he listened to her.

Finally, her advice about making it to top positions was, "Put together a team of people who make up for your deficiencies, share your values, and tell you the absolute unvarnished truth."

Best List of Work Basics—Ever

★ ★ ★

Suzanna Sugarman
CPA and retired real estate developer

Just prior to completing an MBA, my dad (a very successful businessman) gave me some sage advice, which I added to a list I'd been keeping from a couple of my first bosses, who were terrific mentors.

- Get a job working for the best firm and seek out a mentor.
- Be a sponge. Listen, ask questions, and learn as much as possible. Then use this knowledge as a springboard to catapult your career to the next level.
- Focus on what can be achieved, NOT on the unrealistic. The old saying that the devil is in the details is so true.
- Be fully prepared, anticipate questions, be ready with the answers. If you don't know the answer, don't make it up— ask if you can

get back to them with the answer.
- Be direct, focused, positive, and creative. (Oh, and punctual!)
- Think and work smart. Accomplish what needs to get done in fewer hours than other people take.
- Hire the very best team. Surround yourself with experienced winners to meet goals and guarantee success in any business endeavor.

Say Yes . . . and Stretch

★ ★ ★

I began my interview with Lynne Doughtie, U.S. Chairman and CEO, KPMG, by asking about the conference. "We went to major employers and asked for them to send us two women who were close to winning executive jobs. We designed this conference to get them there. We want more women in the C-suite. And that's why we're all here."

I asked Doughtie, who leads 30,000 partners and professionals across the United States, about women and self-confidence. "To see their self-confidence ebb is a common dilemma for women during their careers. They hold back because they think they have to be perfect."

Many studies have revealed that women are less likely to express interest in a new role unless they meet every one of the criteria for the job. Men, on the other hand, still apply even when they meet only half of the criteria.

So, how do women who have accomplished great things in their lives handle those moments when they feel less than certain? Says Doughtie, "I have learned through the years that the way for me to build my confidence is to say yes and then just jump in and do it . . . and impress myself! If you are feeling totally secure, you probably aren't stretching yourself enough, and that means you're not growing!"

You Can Always Change Your Mind

★ ★ ★

Susan Robinson
Human Resources Consultant

Many years ago, when I was struggling with a decision, my father said to me, "Susan, you can always change your mind."

I'm a structured, pragmatic, determined, and focused person who doesn't like to make mistakes. Knowing that I could change my mind and it would not change my character gave me freedom, confidence, strength.

The circumstances were that someone close to me made a decision I was not sure I could ever accept. Granted, it was not illegal, it was not immoral; but, at the same time, it went against my personal beliefs at the time. It was a decision that affected many people, and it was something I would never have done myself. Yet I risked being estranged from this person for a very long time, if not forever. I thought if I "gave in" and accepted this person's decision, it would mean that I agreed with the decision.

My father saw that I was having a hard time with it. After a lengthy discussion, he hugged me and said those wise and freeing words: "Susan, you can always change your mind." I can still see that scene in my mind some twenty years later. At that moment, I "got it." It made me realize that accepting did not mean agreeing. Accepting did not mean I had to like the decision. I had confused values with opinions. I had an opinion about this decision, but I had no real evidence that my opinion was well founded. My wise father taught me you can change your opinion, but your values are like the stripes on a tiger; they never change. I could still be a woman of my word and change my mind.

In the mid-'90s after I had just finished my master's, I was offered a job at a different company. The position was in management, a promotion and big step up for me with a great title to go along with it. This is what I had dedicated all the time and effort in pursuing an advanced degree for. It would mean leaving a company where I was happy, even though I was not making nearly the going rate for someone with an advanced degree. It would also mean leaving longtime friends and an industry I was well suited for.

Now, I have a fairly strict personal work ethic. I don't job-hop. I am super-loyal to whatever company I work for. I carefully analyze decisions, weigh the pros and cons, and pride myself in thinking things through thoroughly. After all that, I accepted the offer.

Two short months into this job, I knew I had made a big mistake. I didn't respect the industry, I didn't like the way they did business, and I was unhappy. So unhappy, in fact, I would eat lunch in my car, in the office parking lot, just to get out of the environment. I was going to have to swallow my pride, admit that all my careful and calculated assessments of this move were wrong, and ask for my old job back or, at the very least, something similar.

Once again, my father's words came back to me. Changing my mind, admitting I made a mistake, would not tarnish my character. It gave me freedom, confidence, and strength to pick up the phone, call my previous manager, and ask if I could come back. (It is important to note that this was a family-owned large company run by a very patriarchal second-generation founder. He made it clear that if you quit, you were not welcome back.) The "rules" were waived and I was hired back in a new role that was tailor-made for me to reflect my master's-level skill set. I continued to work there for fifteen years.

> I am glad that I paid so little attention to good advice; had I abided by it I might have been saved from some of my most valuable mistakes.
>
> —Edna St. Vincent Millay
>
> Pulitzer Prize–winning American poet

Be Resourceful

★ ★ ★

Daisy McCarty
Founder, Brand Message Clarity

The best business advice I've ever received was from B2B sales coach Chaz Horn. Two simple words: "Be resourceful." That's been absolutely essential in today's rapidly changing marketplace where what worked last year in terms of getting new clients might not work tomorrow. It has helped me greatly as I've changed the focus of my business and the way I go about filling my sales pipeline. Now, instead of feeling frustrated or discouraged when things change, I see it as an opportunity to practice resourcefulness. It turns business into a game that I know I can win!

> Find someone who likes to get things done, and help that person.
> —Kris Manos
> Corporate Director, KeyCorp

A Turning Point

★ ★ ★

In my interview with Suzy Whaley—soon to begin her role as the first female president of the Professional Golfers' Association (PGA) of America—she surprised me when she told me she had no intention of becoming a golf professional.

"I was going to go to law school. But I played some good golf. I played well in two LPGA events as an amateur and came to the attention of some people who wanted to send me to [the PGA] tour school. So, I called my mother and told her I was going to tour school—not law school. My mother took the news well. 'That's fantastic! You can always go to law school.'"

Soon Suzy and her mom were on their way to Sweetwater, Texas, where Suzy secured her tour card on her first try. Shortly thereafter, though, she hit a bad streak: She missed three qualifying cuts, lost her tour card, and made only $2,000 for the year. Suzy was distraught.

Then the turning point came. Suzy told me her mistake had been to simply rely on her natural talent. In taking her abilities for granted she had ignored the discipline it takes to be a better golfer.

Suzy was determined to do what it took to get back on

the LPGA tour! It took her two long years—waitressing to support herself—but she earned her tour card and the privilege of competing again.

As she put it, that was "one of the best moments" of her career. After all, golf is a game of fundamentals that must become habits. (Kind of like life!)

Slow Down

★ ★ ★

Jennifer Walker
Senior Vice President Marketing, VisitCalifornia.org

While it may seem basic, even laughable, at first glance, Bob Lander [longtime CEO of VisitAustin.org] gave me the simple but powerful business advice to "Slow down and think." In a world—and in my case, discipline—that often expects nimble pivots and quick if not reactive/ASAP responses, slowing down to take the time to think before you respond or react to a situation has proved to me to be the most sage advice.

When I find myself frazzled at the end of the day, I go home and "marinate on it." I often find a solution, response, or idea that evening that's different from the one I had even an hour prior. Because of that, I believe this skill has saved me from many small mistakes, misinterpretations, or simply poor management or professionalism on my part. I think about the implications of my response. Who may need to be involved? Or perhaps even: Are there different solutions or approaches to the problem at hand? In this reactive, "always-on" world in which we live and work, taking the time to slow down and simply think should be a nurtured skill in every employee . . . and in every relationship, for that matter.

Crowdsource Your Ideas

★ ★ ★

Sara Canaday
Leadership keynote speaker, author, and executive coach

During my years as a corporate manager, I had a few occasions when I was asked to brief or present a business case to the executive team. I knew these executives didn't miss a beat. My data had to withstand extreme dissection; my message had to be on point and my delivery succinct and compelling. So, I spent hours perfecting my pitch, points, and polish.

When I was finally ready to address the group, my then boss urged me to visit with one or more of the executives individually before accepting a place on the agenda. I thought her advice was sound and that I might get some buy-in for my pitch. What I didn't expect was that my tightly organized and thoroughly researched presentation would evolve based on some simple but impactful insights from the people I approached.

Her recommendation is one that I still follow today, whether I'm presenting a keynote or a talk for fifteen people. I still prepare thoroughly, but I get stakeholder input before and after developing my presentation so that my final message is credible and relevant.

> At my first job as an independent researcher at MIT Lincoln Laboratory, they told me I could work on most anything, but not what I knew something about. That is actually very good advice to a young person starting a career, because you bring new ideas to the field.
>
> —Mildred S. Dresselhaus
> Professor Emerita of Physics and Electrical Engineering, MIT

Start Fresh Tomorrow

★ ★ ★

Before interviewing Nancy Kerrigan at the KPMG Women's Leadership Summit, I was in the audience for the session titled "Resilience and Grit: The Making of a Champion," moderated by NBC golf announcer Dan Hicks. The two-time Olympic medalist and U.S. national figure skating champion spoke about her early years learning to skate, as part of that panel. Here are my takeaways from Kerrigan's comments on stage as well as our one-on-one conversation afterward.

"My skating lessons and coaching fees put a real strain on our family's household budget." Kerrigan's father, a welder, often worked three jobs to fund her skating career, and he operated the "Zamboni" at the local rink in exchange for Nancy's lessons. As a result she felt a "deep responsibility" to make the most of their investment in her.

Nancy was on a strict regimen: She would get up early and practice each morning before school and leave early from school to practice with her coach. She was "all in" to perfect the demanding moves required to compete. Sometimes that proved to be frustrating, though. She remembers one particular practice session when she could not get the move right. Again and again she tried to hit the mark but couldn't. That's when her coach said, "Just go home."

"I was shocked by the advice," she said. "In my mind, it smacked of giving up." But the coach assured her that sometimes she just needed to back off, give it a rest, and start fresh the next day.

"It was good advice for skating and for life," she conceded.

When I asked her later to probe deeper into the subject of advice, she smiled and said, "I've gotten lots of advice, especially about parenting." (Kerrigan and her husband have three children.) When that happens, she's "learned to graciously accept the advice, and let the giver know I will mull it over. Then I use what I can, and let the other stuff go."

Guess What? It's Up to You

★ ★ ★

Diana Holford
Managing Director, Jones Lang LaSalle (formerly The Staubach Company)

Our office in Pittsburgh was in One Oxford Centre on the thirty-third floor. One day my boss called me into his office and told me to look out the window.

"Look down on Grant Street. See the courthouse? Go over one block; do you see the green awning on the next building?"

I located the green awning and enthusiastically said I did.

"That is the gift store. If you are looking for a gift, that is where you can get one. Here in this office, there are no gifts. You have to earn everything."

His words truly changed my mindset. I had been back on my heels, not up on my toes. From that day forward I took much more initiative and control over my work.

Stretch

★ ★ ★

Grace Lieblein
Retired Vice President of General Motors and current member of Southwest Airlines' Board of Directors

One of the best pieces of career advice that I received was to take on stretch assignments and move outside my comfort zone. It took me a while to really learn this one, but I eventually did. Midway in my engineering career, the head of Engineering asked me to take on an assignment in an area where I didn't have much experience. My immediate thought was that I wasn't qualified, and I told him so. He assured me that he was confident I could do the job and encouraged me to stretch. I did take the role, was successful, and learned a lot. He was right.

A few years later, this happened again. New role, me doubtful, he encouraging. I took that position, and it was not only a great experience but a career turning point as well. It was also a turning point for my confidence.

After that, I no longer stepped back from new and different positions. That led me to move from being an Engineering leader to the President of General Motors Mexico and then the President of GM Brazil, along with other great opportunities. I learned to believe in my capabilities and in my ability to adapt.

I also learned that my real growth, both personally and professionally, occurred when I did step out of my comfort zone. I am thankful to that leader who helped me learn this, and I've shared his advice with many others I've mentored.

Customer Service 101

★ ★ ★

Melissa Gilbride
Aviator specialist

What I've learned working at Jets.com is this: "It's not the problem itself, but how you handle the problem that makes clients love you." Dealing with aviation, we have a lot of issues arise that are out of our control, such as an unexpected mechanical issue or a weather issue. When clients are paying top dollar for private jets, they expect a seamless experience, and while they understand unforeseen problems may come up, how you remedy the situation is really what they remember. Sometimes it can be as easy as offering free catering.

If I do everything in my power to recover the situation and listen to my clients' needs, [it can take them to] "Oh well, it happens."

Get In over Your Head

★ ★ ★

Shon Medin
Chief Communications Officer, Breakthrough, and Recruiter & Social Media Specialist, Xylo Technologies

Some of the best business advice I ever received was "Get in over your head" or have "OSMs," which stands for "Oh S*** Moments," because it will be in those moments that you

1. Are forced to face your fears.
2. Learn how to manage time and stress.
3. Experience the most growth and adventure.

Life is something that is meant to be lived. We're supposed to reach our maximum potential in pursuit of our dreams, passions, and ideas.

Truly, the sky is the limit. Things are only impossible until you find a way, and getting in over my head often helps me to find those ways, ask those questions, and get the resources to accomplish what I desire to do. I go into everything now with the mindset of "I don't care if I fail because I will learn, but I am determined to succeed!" It has removed the stress from everything and helped me to step up to more challenges, ask for the impossible, and never give up, because I will make it in the end.

Befriend Your Banker

★ ★ ★

Margo Portillo
Cofounder, Tramex Travel

Early on, I heard two different pieces of business advice that have stuck with me over the years.

The first was from my father while I was still in college. "Never work for the state or federal government, and if you can, work for yourself."

The second was when my husband and I first started our own business, a friend told us this: "The most important relationship you need to have is with your banker. When starting out, you need to interview bankers and figure out which bank and officer will be the best fit. If you do not have this established relationship at the start, your chances of growing and prospering your business with be greatly diminished."

Through the years, our business changed and grew rapidly, and the advice held true. It was critically important to have a banker who knew us inside and out, who was there to help support us in the growth with needed capital.

> Wall Street is the only place that people ride to in a Rolls-Royce to get advice from those who take the subway.
>
> —Warren Buffett
> Business magnate, philanthropist

Lead by Example

★ ★ ★

Steve Amos
Founder and Executive Officer, HealthCode

The best advice ever given to me on the business front was not spoken. It was learned—by watching Jon Colby, my first boss after I graduated with an MBA from Wake Forest's School of Business. Jon was International Marketing Director for Homelite Textron. Always there early, he never asked someone else to do anything he would not do. If there was weekend or late-night work, Jon was right there, alongside, working with us.

> Be so good they can't ignore you.
> —Steve Martin

Listen to the Music

★ ★ ★

Mark Cleveland
Serial entrepreneur, cofounder, Hytch LLC

Basketball great Bill Walton suffered through debilitating and life-threatening spinal surgeries. In the midst of that he even thought of committing suicide. How could he get through all that? What was missing?

"I forgot to listen to music," he said to me while we were working out together at his home in San Diego. He soon corrected that and found that taking time out and really listening to music reprogrammed his mind, body, and spirit.

We were talking about small business challenges and life in a leadership role. I paid attention to that advice. When Hytch seems impossible, when everyone is skeptical about my choices and decisions, when I need inspiration or insulation, I listen to music. Music is math. It's the language of the universe. It's, frankly, reprogramming me with joy and creativity as I go about tackling my challenges.

> This is my advice to entrepreneurs. It's easy to give up, but believe in your ideas. Surround yourself with people you respect and are smarter than you.
>
> —Brian Lee
> Ernst & Young's 2014 Emerging Entrepreneur of the Year award

JILL GRIFFIN

Be Prepared

★ ★ ★

Justin Alexander
Implementation specialist, AutoAlert, LLC

The best advice I have received was "Always bring a pen."

I remember my first job interview well. I was sixteen and had absolutely no idea what to expect. I interviewed at a local car dealership for a porter position to work after school and on Saturdays, mainly moving and washing vehicles on the lot. The hiring manager knew this would be my first real job and was easy enough on me during the interview. After some back and forth, he offered me the position and handed me the offer to sign.

> Gayle Lanier, Senior Vice President, Duke Energy, told Business Insider's Richard Feloni that the best advice she's ever had from a mentor is: "'Never let other people take credit for your work.' I've learned to be more vocal and make sure I'm heard."

I looked back at him and asked to borrow a pen. He laughed and said, "This one's free. But in the future always bring a pen." This sounds simple enough but has really resonated on a larger scale the more my professional career has grown.

As an Eagle Scout I heard the phrase "Be Prepared" thousands of times but never really thought how it would affect me on a daily basis. Looking ahead and preparing yourself for what is to come is by far one of the best ways to stand out. By preparing for impacts and scenarios, you can quickly find solutions while others are left scratching their heads. In business, everything is a negotiation. And the best way to win a negotiation? Be better prepared than the person sitting across the table from you.

Show Up

★ ★ ★

Ann Kasper
Fashion brand consultant, coach, and speaker

My father always spoke to me about commitment and the importance of understanding the hard work that other people put in. That when you are asked to support something you ALWAYS show up. One way to acknowledge the work people do is first and foremost by showing up and showing up on time. I am reminded of this every day, and I can still hear him talking to me.

Early in my career I worked for Eileen Fisher, the clothing designer. I was fortunate to work for her in the early growth years of her business. I reported to her and always enjoyed our conversations and her observations. I was young, full of drive, and very direct. She told me one day that I should remember that the journey was part of the process. Not everyone would make the same decisions but they would all come to the destination. My role was to guide them, but I should be open to the ideas of the team and allow everyone to find their own path to the destination. Setting the goals and making sure everyone had access to what they needed to hit those goals was not the same for everyone. This perspective was huge for me and truly a gift, as I use it and have used it in all capacities of my life.

> Never give up. Today is hard, tomorrow will be worse, but the day after tomorrow will be sunshine.
>
> —Jack Ma
> Founder of Alibaba

Trust Your Gut

★ ★ ★

Dr. Lee Mathias
Independent chairman, company director, and bio-med investor

Trust your gut! Of course, for me, any decision I make is based on knowledge, skill, and experience, so when the time comes there is rarely anything visceral about the process. But, on occasion, it is the EQ (Emotional Quotient) that confirms the direction I take.

In 2016, for instance, I was involved in a huge investment decision. I was not comfortable from the beginning, but all the [supporting] information given by the executive stacked up. The decision was made for phase one of the project, which had problems from the start. Luckily, by the next off-ramp I was better prepared and managed to pull the project. If I'd trusted my gut from the beginning, it would have saved time and money.

> If you don't like the road you're walking, start paving another one.
>
> —Dolly Parton

Make a Plan

★ ★ ★

Diana Keller
Cofounder, Shelton-Keller Group

I had been working in accounting for a chemical company for five years and was not happy with the type of work I was doing. I liked being with people, so I thought the best career move was to go into sales.

A gentleman I knew, who was a successful salesman himself, told me: "Everything you touch, smell, see, and hear, has to be sold!" He also said that 80 percent of "sellers" do not follow through. His advice was: "Plan your work and work your plan."

It was great advice. I changed careers and found my love for people and design in the commercial furnishings busi-

> The most valuable advice I can give is plan for your success. Write down your ideal goal, creating checkpoints for yourself along the way that align with the end goal. Set up rewards for achieving both little victories and big ones.
> —Hilary Knight
> Olympic gold medal champion, U.S. women's national ice hockey team, and speaker at KPMG Women's Leadership Summit, June 2018

ness. I became a manufacturer's representative, selling to furniture dealers, which gave me the insight into the contract furnishings industry in which I am now invested as a dealer-owner. I realized I needed to be a "seller" on the dealer side of this business (which gave me control of the sale).

A friend once told me this industry is like Hotel California: Once you get in, you can never leave!

After thirty-five years, it's now all about mentoring the ones behind us in their own personal and professional growth. It creates great people to manage and run our businesses. In helping and supporting others, our own areas of growth emerge. It's a win-win for everyone involved.

> You never need to feel like you have to be the smartest person in the room. Building a good team requires you to hire people that may know more in a certain subject than you do. Find individuals who have a diverse set of skills and experiences and feel free to rely on them for advice and responsibilities.
>
> —Heather Robertson
> Owner of Expedia Cruise Ship Centers of Mill Creek

> A mentor is someone who is willing to give you advice that isn't in the best interest for them. It takes a real mentor to put you first.
>
> —Caroline Ghosn
> CEO and Founder, Levo

Follow the Light

★ ★ ★

Molly Fitzpatrick
Boulder County (Colorado) Clerk and Recorder

Don't worry about what you will do next. If you take one step with all the knowledge you have, there is usually just enough light shining to show you the next step."

This advice was given to me by someone I admire very much —Mary Young, a community leader and member of the Boulder City Council. She sent me this quotation by Mardy Murie when I was deciding whether or not to run for public office, for the role of Boulder County Clerk and Recorder. There were long lists of reasons to run, including passion for the mission, the right skill set for the job, and the positive impact this role has on the community.

But, I never thought that running for public office was something I would do. It was never in my plan, and anyone who knows me knows that I like plans and sticking to them.

I kept returning to Murie's inspiring words when I was making the decision. I found a tremendous amount of comfort in them and gained so much clarity from them. I think there's so much resistance to change and making a detour from "the plan," but oftentimes changes in a plan can be your most important decisions and can bring you tremendous amounts of growth, learning, and opportunity.

> In her tender, moving tribute *The Seasons of My Mother: A Memoir of Love, Family, and Flowers* (Atria Books, 2018), Marcia Gay Harden credits her mother with launching her career. Though Beverly wasn't the stereotypical stage mom, she nonetheless had a realistic view of her daughter's unique talent. And her daughter's self-professed "stubborn insecurity" as a new college graduate armed with a bachelor's degree in theater.
>
> When Marcia was visiting her parents one weekend in their home near Washington, D.C., Beverly showed Marcia "an article about auditions for a local production of Neil Simon's *I Ought to Be in Pictures*." The actor "insisted" it was a musical; the agent "gently offered" to make a phone call to see whether it was, indeed, a musical. The actor grunted her approval.
>
> What happened next? "It wasn't a musical. I auditioned and got my first professional theater part. What's more, I received good reviews and won an award. More plays and good reviews followed. Somehow, my mother knew that if she just got me to the edge, I'd fly."

To me, this quote signified that you should never make a decision out of fear, because enough doors will always be open to lead you forward. And this is exactly what happened for me throughout this process. Ever since I made the decision to run, every door that could have opened has opened and signaled that this was the right step. I am trusting that throughout this process—and, hopefully, into the role—there will always be enough light shining to show me the next step. So far, there has been!

> **Attitude is a little thing that can make a big difference.**
> **—Winston Churchill**

If You Knew You Could Not Fail

★ ★ ★

Christopher Avery, PhD
CEO, Partnerwerks, Inc., best-selling author, international speaker

I met Patti Danos, publicist for my first book, at a dinner meeting in Chicago, her home. I was there on business.

Patti gave me a present, a small and heavy package. Opening it I found a metal bar, five inches long, a little more than an inch tall, and half an inch wide. On one side was a small question mark, inviting me to turn it over. On the other side were these words: "What would you attempt to do if you knew you could not fail?"

(This quote, by the way, is widely attributed to Robert Schuller, but he was simply paraphrasing the words of the poet Robert Frost, who wrote, "How many things would you attempt if you knew you could not fail?")

It took my breath away then, as it does now. What am I avoiding because I'm afraid of failure?

Too much!

Yes, that little metal bar—made of pewter, I think—lives

on my desk or somewhere close by where I see it every day.

When I have a decision in front of me and my spirit says "Go for it," but my internal saboteurs say, "But what if you're not good enough?" that little question reminds me that it is far better to have tried and fallen short than to have never tried at all. "You never learn less," the great genius R. Buckminster Fuller taught me. One way to translate that is that there is no true failure, only learning.

One such decision that stands out is my decision to leave behind a perfectly good market position as a teamwork guy and dedicate myself to mastering and promoting The Responsibility Process worldwide. This was 2006. My 2001 book, *Teamwork Is an Individual Skill*, was selling well. My work in collaborative leadership was in demand. And yet, I knew that The Responsibility Process was the most important information I know and had to offer.

But it seemed so hard. There was no ready-made market. I would have to create one. And that meant I would have to create a need, then fulfill it.

"What would you attempt to do if you knew you could not fail?"

So I began. I set a purpose, a vision, a mission, a set of values. I began to speak and write. Then some seminars followed. Individuals started asking how they could get access to this amazing material (so far it was only available inside of corporations in my leadership development and culture change programs). So I founded The Leadership Gift Program, an eLearning community with an exceptional reputation for results now serving leaders and coaches worldwide.

The Responsibility Process now has thousands of fans all over the world. There is a huge tribe helping with the purpose and vision of changing conversations everywhere about what responsibility is and how it works in the mind. Search on my name and the word "responsibility" and you'll see how wide the reach is in just eleven years.

In my twenty-seven years in business, I've fallen on my face ten thousand times. I've learned and relearned expensive lessons over and over. But I've never failed because I've never quit. And the universe keeps supporting me.

Now it's your turn. What would you attempt to do if you knew you could not fail?

> Give yourself permission to challenge assumptions, to look at the world with fresh eyes, to experiment, to fail, to plot your own course, and to test the limits of your abilities. In fact, that's exactly what I wish I had known when I was twenty, and thirty, and forty—and what I constantly need to remind myself at fifty.
>
> —Tina Seelig
> Executive director, Stanford Technology Ventures Program, author of *inGenious* and *Creativity Rules*

Make a Career Change

★ ★ ★

Dorian Alexander
Estimator, project manager

In March 2014 I was working as a concrete superintendent at a large company. At that time, I had been with the company for more than twelve years. As the superintendent, my responsibilities included—but were not limited to—overseeing every component of the job, from award through its completion. I was both successful in this position and confident in my abilities to continue to assist the company's growth.

The downside of the position, however, was the amount of travel required for my continued success. I found myself traveling in excess of 200 days a year. My wife and I had just had a new baby, and we also had a very active twelve-year-old daughter who had an extensive list of activities that required our constant involvement.

I realized very quickly it was time to begin the process of making a career change. Soon after my search began, I was offered a position as an estimator with a Kansas City asphalt and concrete contractor. The prospect of the new job was both encouraging and terrifying; there were so many unknowns, and as with any change, I was very apprehensive.

While I was still debating the change, I happened to see the father of a good friend of mine. I spoke with him at length regarding my impending decision, weighing the pros and cons. I was hopeful someone I respected so much as a successful businessman, husband, and father would be able to assist me in heading in the right direction. He assured me that each time he had been in the process of making a career move he had likewise been apprehensive and hesitant. He was confident in both my work ability and my work ethic and advised me that as long as I continued with the core principles I was raised with, I would be successful in any endeavor. He strongly urged me to make the move and further assured me that, in time, I would see the benefit of my leap of faith.

I will soon be celebrating my fourth anniversary with the new company, and my decision to move has proved itself right on more occasions than I can count. Not only was it a financial gain, the travel is virtually nonexistent and I have both the respect and the autonomy in my new position to take it as far as I can see. As with most significant life choices, I believed in myself, my ability, and my family, and all of this combined to form not only a successful professional life, but a better home life as well.

> My success was due to good luck, hard work, and support and advice from friends and mentors. But most importantly, it depended on me to keep trying after I had failed.
>
> —Mark Warner
> Senior U.S. Senator from Virginia

FOLLOW THESE LEADERS

Don't Do It

★ ★ ★

Mark Skoggard
Retired executive

I was a year into planning and putting in place a rooftop restaurant concept in Winston-Salem, North Carolina. I had gotten a master's certificate in food service management from the Cornell School of Hotel Administration, located a property, and identified my chef. I thought I was planning the risk out of the project—covering all the bases.

As was my habit, I checked in with Joe Gangloff, my mentor of many years. I had worked for him at R. J. Reynolds and VF Corp. I often sought his opinion and greatly respected his advice. I was expecting, "Good job, Mark. You've really thought of everything."

> Twenty years ago, Ona Porter, a consultant from New Mexico, told me, "No success at work is worth failure at home." I have followed this advice and shared it with many people ever since.
> —Earl Maxwell, CEO, St. David's Foundation

As was his habit, he took several days to get back to me. What I received then was a very well-thought-out critique of the restaurant business. Joe had researched business morbidity factors. "Why would you enter a business with an 80 percent failure rate within three years?" he wondered. He brought up that people problems abound in the industry —turnover, tardiness, theft. On and on he went with very little, if anything, positive to say. To put it succinctly, "Don't do it" was his advice. I was dumbfounded.

"Joe," I said, "I'm really deep into this project. It's going to be very hard to pull the plug on it." I could see him shaking his head and thinking, "You stubborn SOB. Don't make me have to tell you I told you so."

I opened the restaurant. In the first place, I had made a particularly poor partner decision—generally the number 1 or 2 killer of restaurants. After forty-eight months in business, I sold the assets at a loss. Although revenue was $1.2 million at the time, the overhead equation was way off base. I couldn't get cash flow to carry us through the cold months. You may remember the story about the melon salesman who sold each melon at a dollar loss and wanted a bigger truck? That was similar to my situation. In addition, the physical plant was just too big.

It took me a while to lick my wounds, swallow my pride, and apologize to Joe for not following his counsel. To his credit, he accepted my mea culpa and, being the good U.S. Marine he is, simply said, "Semper Fi."

The biggest lesson I learned from being a lawyer was not to be afraid to argue. It's not the end of the world for someone to disagree with me. . . . Women have to be bolder about voicing an opinion, because half the time men are wrong too.

—Sarah Albrey
Executive Vice President of Original Programming for TNT

Girls Can Do Anything

★ ★ ★

Carol Thompson
Former President, Austin Chamber of Commerce, executive coach, and mentor

When I was about six years old in 1947, I was helping my father inventory parts at our family-owned Gloucester Machine Shop. He serviced fishing boats in this historic Massachusetts seaport city.

One day when I completed my task, my father looked at me with a smile and said, "Always remember, girls can do anything."

I took his words of advice to heart. From selling Girl Scout cookies door-to-door to being chosen to be a graduation speaker in high school, I was on my way. In the years that followed, my businesses ranged from computer franchises to two technology recruiting businesses. These business connections, my networking, and the prodding of good friends led me to be nominated as the third woman in 117 years to be Board Chair of the Austin Chamber of Commerce.

In that position, I helped lead our first economic development trip to Silicon Valley. Being Board Chair provided me "a seat at the table"—several tables, in fact. A local bank president nominated me for a seat on the Federal Reserve Board San Antonio branch. I was the first woman since 1926 to serve on that particular board.

After that the Dean of UT's Cockrell School of Engineering asked me to serve on their Advisory Board. In 1993, I founded the Young Women's Alliance, which focuses on training recent college graduates to lead, network, and volunteer in their communities.

Throughout all my life, I have learned two other key pieces of advice in addition to my father's affirmation:

> All of us might be more inclined to ask for help if we treat the word "ask" as an acronym that stands for Acquire. Specific. Know-How. Right? I'm pretty sure that authors Sally Helgesen and Marshall Goldsmith would agree with me. In fact, in their new book, *How Women Rise: Break the 12 Habits Holding You Back from Your Next Raise, Promotion, or Job* (2018, Hachette Books), they include a chapter titled "Don't Do It Alone." They admonish overworked women to enlist help from others. And they underscore that yes, how you ask for help or feedback is important; but, how you respond to the help and feedback you receive should be just as intentional as how you ask for it.
> —Jill Griffin

- Humor saves steps and, in fact, can save years.
- Remember to ask for help.

> Be willing to relocate. Soak up the culture in every position. Build relationships at every stop.
>
> —Cathey Lowe, CPA
> Corporate Director, The New Home Company

> No one can make you feel inferior without your consent
>
> —Eleanor Roosevelt

Family Lessons

★ ★ ★

Gylfi Skarphéđinsson
Management Executive, Head of Logistics and Telephone Services at Landspitali University Hospital

The first advice I would pass along is the so-called Golden Rule, found in many religions: "Treat others as you wish to be treated." This is simple advice but not always easy to follow. Looking back, I feel I could have applied this rule more often and almost everything I regret in life is more or less a result of my forgetting to apply this rule in my interaction with people. Imagine a world where everyone lived by this rule! That would be something different from what we are experiencing in the world today.

The second word of advice comes from my grandson. When he was four years old, he said to me once, "Granddad, when I grow old I want to by just like you; a bit of a fool." This melted my heart, not that it needs much melting when my grandchildren are concerned. What he said is not advice, per se, but more of a result of advice I got years back. "Always remember to be yourself." In my language [Icelandic] this is called "to come to the door clothed as you are." Of course, we all unintentionally take on different behaviors in our day-to-day life. I don't behave in quite the same way in my workplace as I do at home. But I have always tried to be myself and not to take myself too seriously, avoiding stepping into some role to project something I am not. Sometimes that has resulted in me thinking at the end of the day that I shouldn't really have said this or done that, worrying what people might think of me. But it must be exhausting to do the opposite—always trying to be someone else.

And the third word of advice is something I got in my management studies: At the end of each day, try to recap the day. What do you think you did well and what do you think you could have handled better? I often forget to do this, but when I do, I feel that it does me good and makes me better. This has evolved through the years. I also try to think of what I am grateful for. Before I go to sleep, I close my eyes and think of all the things I am grateful for: Having met my wife, my family, having a roof over my head, having this fantastic job where I make a difference every day, for financial stability, good health, and for having been born in this fantastic, beautiful country of Iceland where we have a low crime rate, pure water, and peace.

I think it is healthy for everyone to acknowledge the things you have, because it not only makes you grateful and humble but also makes you think of those who are less fortunate and who don't have what you might take for granted.

Do Something

★ ★ ★

Fay Evans-Martin
Retired business executive, Austin, Texas

My first full-time job after college was in banking, and my first boss gave me some advice that I still remember and appreciate. The larger bank that I worked for provided services to smaller banks in an arrangement called "correspondent banking," and our office was the center of this activity. My boss told me if I received a request from a customer bank and he was not available for advice, that "doing something is always better than doing nothing." He added that there was almost nothing that I could do that couldn't be fixed, but giving the impression that we were incapable or unwilling to handle the needs of our customers could be disastrous to the business relationship.

This advice served me well in that first job and also gave me the confidence to trust my instincts and the knowledge accumulated on the job to make informed decisions. Later, as an accounting manager and controller, I felt my most important job was to train employees to make the best decisions they could, using the best information available.

> One of the most important things about leadership is that you have to have the kind of humility that will allow you to be coached.
>
> —Jim Yong Kim
> President, World Bank

> I walk slowly, but I never walk backward.
>
> —Abraham Lincoln

Marketing Matters

★ ★ ★

Dorie Clark
Adjunct Professor, Duke University Fuqua School of Business, consultant, and keynote speaker

An early piece of business advice that made a difference for me was from Jake, an older entrepreneur who had served on the board of the nonprofit I was leading before I started my consulting business. Jake had cashed out successfully and was now an angel investor, and he loved sharing his business knowledge. He told me early on that I should devote at least 25 percent of my time to marketing and business development, and I tried to follow his advice carefully.

In fact, it became the cornerstone of my later efforts in content creation, which helped me take my business to a new level of success. It's incredibly hard for new business owners or entrepreneurs, once they start making money, to willfully turn down business in favor of undertaking longer-term brand-building activities like writing articles or books. But, it's necessary for continued growth. Jake's advice helped me see the importance of preparing for the future, and it's served me well.

Find a Mentor

★ ★ ★

Tom Noonan
CEO, VisitAustin.org

I took my dad's advice: When you are starting out find two to three mentors and keep those mentors throughout your career.

And the payback is to be a mentor as often as possible. I relish the opportunity to be that role in others' lives. It really is the greatest gift.

> As you get older, you grow and mature, and that should never stop. As soon as you stop growing, you're done living. I'll always be growing, forever learning, forever taking in advice from people I deeply respect.
>
> —Odell Beckham, Jr.
> 2014 NFL Offensive Rookie of the Year, NY Giants wide receiver

Hard on the Task, Easy on the People

★ ★ ★

Vicki Knox West
Director, Center for Professional Sales, and Gowens Professor of Excellence in Business Administration, Texas State University

During harvest season in the Midwest, our farm was a hotbed of activity, with trucks, tractors, hay balers, dogs, horses, and lots of people doing lots of work. The smells of fresh hay were intoxicating. My parents, Roy and Norma Knox, were at the center of it all, directing and working like fools. My sister and I were also very involved, doing a wide range of tasks. There was never enough help, so we hired seasonal workers, who were called "hired hands." It was a descriptive, not a derogatory phrase.

Both of my parents repeatedly said, "Be hard on the task, easy on the people." Also, "Never sit down; keep working. You cannot expect others to work hard if you are a slacker." Being a slacker was the absolute worst way to be described in Midwest farm country.

Around 11:00 each day, my sister and I would jump off

the tractors to go to the kitchen to help our mother serve an enormous hot lunch, which would now be described as a fancy dinner. All the seasonal workers were seated on the lawn around big tables, with white tablecloths. My sister and I were the waitresses, serving food like fried chicken, mashed potatoes, and all the trimmings. We were told to call everyone "sir" and treat them like royalty, which we did.

Because of these teachings, one of our family mottos, three generations later, is still "hard on the task, easy on the people." Yes, it is important to get the task done correctly and on time, and instructions and corrections are necessary, but people need to always be treated with respect and courtesy.

We never had any trouble getting seasonal workers on the farm. Years later, when my father had passed away and my mother was alone on the farm, people would come by to see if she needed anything.

> "I didn't get there by wishing for it or hoping for it, but by working for it."
>
> —Estée Lauder

Assume the Best

★ ★ ★

Wil Carruthers
Retail business analyst

In my three years at Family Dollar, the piece of advice I held on to the most was given to me early on by the SVP of Merchandising Support, Jeff Thomas. A personable leader with years of experience on the operations side of retail, he gave this advice at the end of every town hall he led for our team. It was a key part of "Jeff's Rules." "Assume best intentions." I think the reason I've remembered that advice so vividly (I can still close my eyes and picture him standing up in a room and passionately communicating it to his team members) is because it has helped me keep grounded in how I interpret things, both in professional situations and in personal ones too.

Whether in the workplace among coworkers or at home with family and friends, so many situations pose a risk for unnecessary escalation due to misinterpretation. But, if you "assume best intentions" immediately (until otherwise refuted), this can help you avoid confrontation and mold your image into that of a more positive one. Also, I think mastering this skill can have a positive affect on soft skills, such as working within in a team.

> I think the advice, regardless of gender, is always be open to conversations with people who do things differently than you do. If you're starting to work in tech, talk to the artists, talk to the lawyers, talk to the people who are interested in other things.
>
> —Beth Simone Noveck
> Jerry M. Hultin Global Network Professor, NYU's Tandon School of Engineering

Two Key Words to Never Forget: Collaborate and Listen

★ ★ ★

Todd Coutee
Senior Vice President, Operations, Luby's Fuddruckers Restaurants, LLC

Throughout my twenty-nine-year career, I have had the pleasure of working with some tremendously talented and dedicated team members. Biggest lesson learned? **Collaborate** and **Listen** to hourly staff because they are often closer to the challenges, as well as the solution, than I am!

I was a young manager and in charge of the schedule, which included managing payroll, budgeted hours, and overtime control. The ebb and flow of our business required three daily schedules that constantly needed updating. Communication with the management team and hourly team was paramount. We were in the midst of slower-than-budgeted sales and all I heard was "cut, cut, cut" from my boss. I took out my schedule and started slashing, moving people around to ensure coverage as well as rebuilding the next several days' rotations.

When I began to talk to each team member on the proposed schedule, I heard the grumblings. "My hours are being reduced. I need that money. I don't know that position." Finally, one of our cooks approached me and said, "Mr. Coutee, when we're busy, you need us, right? Well, when things are slow, we need you. Can a few of us sit and discuss how we can work through this?"

I was grateful, confused, upset, but mostly embarrassed because I hadn't considered how the changes would affect employees' livelihoods and families. Their suggestions were incredible and very helpful. Collaborating together, we were able to provide solutions that satisfied everyone.

> "When I [Tory Burch] started a company, . . . my parents said . . . 'thicken your skin,' and . . . 'think of negativity as noise.' That idea has really kept me in a frame of mind where I've been focused on the task at hand and not necessarily on the naysayers. I let my work speak for itself."

Don't make assumptions about people based on what they do, their social status, or how much money they make. Trust and listen to your team, be sincere. They will make you proud!

Discouragement and failure are two of the surest stepping-stones to success.

—Dale Carnegie

Be Visible

★ ★ ★

Kelly A. Colotla, CFA, CMT
Senior Vice President and Portfolio Manager, Investment Management Group, Broadway Bank

For most of my career, I was under the impression that if you got a great education, worked hard, and kept your head down, you would get ahead. But I've realized a couple things:

1. The interviewing that takes place when you're sitting across from a hiring manager is probably the least important variable in getting hired. It's about networking, and if you've run into that manager in the past and talked shop, that person was already forming opinions of you and your capabilities that far outweigh anything else.

2. Even within a company if you're not looking for a new role, being visible internally can change the trajectory of your career. This doesn't necessarily mean tooting your own horn (though that's necessary sometimes); it means looking for opportunities

to sit on company-wide committees, having lunch or coffee with executives (or influential colleagues), investing in projects on your own time.

3. For example, I am a passionate member of Toastmasters and recently spent several weekends researching Bitcoin for a club project. I thought I'd give an internal office presentation on the same topic a couple weeks later. Although that gig fell through, when the CEO heard about my presentation, he asked me to deliver it to the executive team and then to the board of directors. So, I got an audience with the people at the very highest levels of my organization because of a pet project I did on the weekends that didn't even fall into my formal job description. I'll take that trade-off all day long!

> Those who work hard and constantly seek to be visible to their superiors, those who showcase their hard work, are the ones who advance to positions of greater power and responsibility.
>
> —Abhishek Ratna
> Author of *No Parking. No Halt. Success Non Stop!*

Shrug Off Negativity

★ ★ ★

Marsha Jones
Partner, HillCo Partners

The best piece of business advice I have received is along the lines of the following:

Negative people like to sling arrows. People you are moving ahead of like to sling arrows. But if you are working hard and doing it the right way, it means you are always ahead of the negative. And the arrows coming your way might sting a little, but you take them on the backside. There are no vital organs there so it doesn't kill you. It just moves you toward your goal.

> I think that's the single best piece of advice: Constantly think about how you could be doing things better and questioning yourself.
>
> —Elon Musk
> Entrepreneur, engineer, investor

Write Your Leadership Credo

★ ★ ★

Julie Fasone Holder
Founder and CEO, JFH Insights

"Be sure you put your feet in the right place. Then stand firm."

I've thought of those words of Abraham Lincoln often throughout my career. I'd spent twenty-plus years of it in the chemicals division of my company and was suddenly moved to a VP role in another division. As part of my "onboarding," I was given an executive coach. After about 100 days, he made the rounds to talk to my peers, my boss, and my direct reports; then we met. Even though the people in the new division knew of me, they didn't know much about me or what was important to me as a leader. So, my coach suggested that I write a Leadership Credo to communicate my vision and values—how I lead and what was important to me as a leader. It was one of the best management tools I've ever created and used. It had a number of intended and a few unintended consequences.

Taking the time to write down how you lead and how

you want to lead is an excellent discipline for yourself. You are forced to distill your beliefs and values to one piece of paper and to be able to clearly communicate them to others. They become an accountability tool for you and for your organization. Once you write down "I want your feedback so we can get better and do better," you had better be prepared to listen and act if necessary—to hear the good news and the bad and not "kill the messenger." Your organization watches and judges you based on how you authentically live your values.

It also teaches your leaders how you expect them to behave as leaders. I had moved into a hierarchical, authoritarian organization and culture, but that wasn't my style. I expected the leaders working for me to develop a leadership style of collaboration and listening. They understood that I was leading differently and started changing their leadership behaviors. And, most surprisingly (and importantly), they started writing their own credos, aligned with mine, and rolled them down the organization so it became an incredible alignment tool. The fifteen hundred people in my organization had a road map that was easy to understand and follow. Great things happen when organizations are aligned behind leaders.

My first Leadership Credo stood the test of time. I used it in every role I moved into after that. It needed only minor tweaks—if any at all—as I continued to progress in my career. It helped me stay true to my values and beliefs as I rose to roles in the C-suite. Good tools last.

> The biggest piece of advice I have is—listen. Don't jump to the answer or what you think the answer is. The more you listen, the more you learn.
>
> —Tim Ryan
> U.S. Congressman, 13th District of Ohio

Be Open to New People

★ ★ ★

Tissa Richards
Founder and CEO, Network Kinetix

I received excellent advice from a mentor early in my career: Never turn down an introduction, even if you don't see the immediate clear value or it seems orthogonal to where you currently are.

This advice has been beneficial to me in several ways, and its real value has become increasingly clear in recent years. Accepting a wide range of sometimes surprising introductions has:

- Directly expanded my personal first-degree network. It sometimes takes years to understand or leverage the value or contribution of these connections, but ultimately the value becomes apparent.
- Expanded the value and interconnections of my second-degree network. I frequently find that connecting a long-ago introduction to another one of my connections will help add immense value to both of them.

These serendipitous moments have happened enough times for me to know it is not just a coincidence and that there is real value—both intrinsic and tangible—to taking this advice to heart and learning to practice it.

It can be difficult at times. I was initially skeptical: Why would I meet with him or her? I'm busy, and this doesn't dovetail with my immediate strategic or tactical needs or goals. Don't distract me from my immediate successes!

But I stopped and thought about it. The people whom I respect and trust have a reason to introduce me to other people. That reason may only be clear to them. And sometimes, it may only be clear to the Universe. And it may not become clear to any of us for a long time.

So, take the time. Everyone has thirty minutes to meet with someone. And in that time, listen. Ask as many questions as you can. That's how you will understand and synthesize what someone has to offer and what you can learn from them. That's how you can mentally bookmark this new connection for the future.

Today, I marvel that my network is comprised of people—quality, remarkable, "curated" people—in a noticeably broad spectrum of industries and geographies and skill sets.

Another reason you never want to turn down an introduction, no matter how orthogonal it may seem to your path, is because your future path may surprise you. I guarantee you.

I never expected to start a company and move out of Silicon Valley. The seeds I planted along my way and throughout my network through all the years of my career have popped up at just the right places and times in this journey. It's a joy to make a call and reconnect with someone and explain that I've ended up somewhere unexpected and find there are new synergies to explore.

I wouldn't be where I am with the progress of my company and career if I hadn't taken that advice and embraced meeting with and learning from as many unexpected people as I have.

You never know who you'll meet, but trust that it will be for a reason.

Note from Jill: Tissa generously offered her entrepreneur readiness audit, "Are You Ready to Start a Company?" for my use in *Follow These Leaders*. Interested readers can find it in the appendix.

> The most significant barrier to female leadership is the actual lack of females in leadership. The best advice I can give to women is to go out and start something, ideally their own businesses. If you can't see a path for leadership within your own company, go blaze a trail of your own.
>
> —Safra Catz
> CEO, Oracle

Be Inclusive

★ ★ ★

Lauren G. Flanagan
Vice President, USI Insurance Services

David Meguschar, President, Indiana Employee Benefits Practice, USI Insurance Services, has been instrumental in my career success with USI. He is inclusive and a giver, supportive of my growth and of the success of those around me.

In October 2017, Dave asked me to read the book *The Go-Giver: A Little Story about a Powerful Business Idea* by Bob Burg and John David Mann. Dave thought it would be a good book to help launch my career with USI.

The focus of the book is about giving without expecting anything in return. Since I've read it, my entire discipline has been nothing short of a 360-degree change. In fact, my New Year's resolutions were shaped by the stories outlined in the book and are inclusive of family, friends, faith, and business.

While the book was about giving, it taught me an invaluable lesson about inclusion. Inclusion is representative of the five laws portrayed in the book:

- Value
- Compensation
- Influence
- Authenticity
- Receptivity

Focusing on connections and building relationships is an important key to success in business, but it is how I am using the five laws that has changed me. I am now focused on other peoples' interests first in an authentic and receptive way. The result is an inclusive network that places me in the center as an influential partner.

Oprah Winfrey says, "Inclusion is to have a seat at the table where the decisions are being made." *The Go-Giver: A Little Story about a Powerful Business Idea* enhanced the lives of those around me because it changed the person I am.

> "In business it's about people. It's about relationships."
>
> —Kathy Ireland
> Former supermodel turned accomplished entrepreneur

Don't Burn Bridges

★ ★ ★

Mary Scott Nabers
CEO, Strategic Partnerships

My late husband, Lynn Nabers, gave me this advice early in our marriage: "Mary, although you rarely get angry, when you do, you are almost always impulsive. Remember how important it is not to burn bridges. The anger will go away and the bridges not burned will provide a sage route back to someone or someplace."

I realized how important and how true that advice was . . . and since then I have never burned bridges.

> Life isn't about finding yourself. Life is about creating yourself.
>
> —George Bernard Shaw

Honor Wisdom

★ ★ ★

Alisa Cohn
NYC Executive Coach and columnist for Inc.com, Forbes.com, Worth.com

I have been so lucky throughout my life to have had many managers, mentors, and colleagues who have given me great advice.

Two moments stand out.

In my first job out of college my manager was Beth Morgan. She was very encouraging and in so many ways showed me how to be a professional. In my first performance review, she told me I had a lot of potential and that she thought I could be a good manager. Then she told me that I was very analytical and was good at spotting problems. The next step for me was to become more "solutions-oriented"—how would I suggest solving the problems that I identified?

That input was a revelation for me. I had never seen myself as responsible for solutions, so just putting that frame around it was helpful. And it was also helpful to hear that so early in my career. I started looking for solutions and never stopped! This quality has helped me build my career, and I often give others Beth's advice.

The second piece of advice came from "my thirty-year-old-mentor," Dorie Clark. I call her that because I met her when she was thirty. She is no longer that age but she is still (and ever will be!) younger than I am and, candidly, wiser than I am. My relationship with Dorie proves that your mentors don't necessarily have to be older.

Dorie really drove home the point that your network is critical to your success. She taught me that being generous is a good professional strategy and, by the way, also makes you feel good.

Because of Dorie, I have focused on building a network which is wide and deep and diverse. I have also focused on finding various ways to help people in my network and to be available to help them when asked. This has turned out to be a great business strategy. I have met many people and been able to be of service. I have introduced people to each other who have formed valuable friendships and business relationships. I have gotten a lot out of my diverse network. For example, I was nominated to go to TED talks because of someone I had known for years, and I was able to return the favor by giving her daughter some helpful career advice. I have gotten referrals for coaching business, writing opportunities, and interesting event opportunities through the network I've built.

Firing and Hiring

★ ★ ★

Bob Birkmaier
Managing Attorney, Nationwide Insurance (Retired)

When I was about to fire an attorney on my team at Nationwide, I was deeply troubled. My Regional Vice President took me aside and said: "You have given him every chance. He did it to himself. Dismiss him knowing it's the right thing to do."

When I was about to take over a new team of ten attorneys that had been riddled by mismanagement, seven of the ten resigned before I got there. I was disheartened. My Regional Vice President took me aside and counseled me this way: "This is the best thing that could happen to you. Now you can pick many of your own team!"

FOLLOW THESE LEADERS

Meanness Rarely Helps

★ ★ ★

Randy Taylor
Founder and CEO, Pinnergy

One of my mentors was Neal Hawthorn, an attorney and the president of a closely held oil and gas company. Our companies were both investors in an oil and gas project operated by another company. As the project developed, neither of us was pleased with the way things were progressing, particularly with some of the decisions made by the pompous CEO of the operating company.

I told Neal that I had just about had it and was thinking of calling the CEO and giving him a piece of my mind. After I had vented for quite some time to Neal's complete silence, he finally said: "I agree with almost everything you said, and I think you should let him have it. You need to sit down and write him a letter stating all the things he has done wrong, how terrible he is, and how he should fix things immediately. You need to sign the letter, seal it, and have it ready to mail. Then . . . you need to put that letter on the corner of your desk and let it stay there for at least a week. After that, open it and read it again.

Then, tear it up and put it in the trash. You can disagree with him, but you don't have to be disagreeable!"

Neal Hawthorn was a gentleman and a good friend.

> You need to have the advice from experienced people coming from different kinds of educational and other backgrounds, and then you can make a decision. But you need people around you that you trust to give you advice, and you need to make sure that the facts of the case are presented.
>
> —Margrethe Vestager
> European Commissioner for Competition

Find Your Champion

★ ★ ★

Melissa Fudge
General Counsel, Spreadfast Software

I was filling in as the Interim General Counsel at Borland in Silicon Valley before Greg Wrenn took the post. When Greg started, I stayed on to transition. He found that I had learned a lot about the business and had bonded with the team. We got to know each other and found that we worked well together.

As a result, he offered me an Associate General Counsel position. We continued to work together. I actively pursued asking for his guidance on how I could become a General Counsel and he actively provided that guidance.

Our work history enabled Greg's trust and confidence in me to strengthen. He helped me grow by involving me in material transactions, important board meetings, personnel issues, and other regular decisions.

I believe that our approaches as counsel were compatible and similar. We were always on the same page and often got to the same conclusions or recommendations on how to deal with issues. This allowed Greg to effectively delegate to me, which I believe made his job easier and at the same time allowed me to build and strengthen my skills.

Be Happy For Another's Success

★ ★ ★

Ralph Hasson
Senior Vice President, Cybernance Corporation

Early in my first career, I had achieved some recognition for the experience I'd built up, and for the roles I'd held. Yet I saw others—many of whom seemed less qualified or accomplished—being appointed to professional bodies or being asked to speak at conferences. A mentor could see that I was struggling with this dynamic. His advice: "Always be happy for the success of others." That advice freed me, and I've followed it ever since.

I took several things from that piece of wisdom:

> First, one of the keys to success is maintaining a clear focus on your goals, and what you can do to achieve them. Worrying about others, or about what didn't happen for you, only gets in the way.

> Second, others may have success for reasons that may not be obvious, but someone or some collection of folks found that person worthy.

Third, success or accomplishment is hard to achieve—celebrate it any time you see it.

Finally, while envy is crippling, the reverse is true as well—happiness for others leaves you in a much better position to pursue your own goals.

PART TWO

My Customer Loyalty Beginning

★ ★ ★

Like many small towns in the 1960s, my hometown, Marshville, N.C., boasted a busy town square made of mom-and-pop businesses. Guion's Drug Store, Audrey's Dress Shop, Collins Brothers Market and Perkins Dry Cleaners were all own and operated by local people.

Ms. Audrey, Mr. Collins and the others were behind their counters every day serving customers most of the which they knew by name.

We came to these stores as much for the latest news and gossip as for their prescriptions, hamburger and dry cleaning.

By big city standards, our buying choices were limited but we didn't know it. Local businesses satisfied our and needs, and in return, won our loyalty;

For most business—large or small—these good old days are gone forever.

To ensure a dependable clientele and curtail the expense if wooing new customers, businesses must go beyond they usual concerns about customer satisfaction and practice building loyal customer one stage at a time. Social media, Twitter, Instagram and the like can be an immense help but only if you can mature those prospect into loyal customer and advocates.

They results will be
- clients, who will, in turn, because you best advocates
- smaller, new customer costs and,
- a bottom-line you can celebrate.

Customer Loyalty Playbook

★ ★ ★

How many of you, on the first date with the person who's now your spouse, popped the "Will you marry me?" question? Very few. Even if you liked that person a lot you probably wanted more time to get familiar. That's the concept behind my proven loyalty model. Every relationship evolves over time. Some drop off early. Others go the distance.

This is true in any relationship you build, be it business or personal.

I've devised six relationship stages:

> Suspect—Prospect—First-Time Customer—
> Repeat Customer—Client—Advocate

Your customers aren't just the folks who push a cart full of goods up to the checkout counter or hit "one click" to buy your wares on Amazon.com. Your peers, your supervisors, your sponsors, your network are all your "customers," too, in the sense that you want to listen to what they need and to give them your very best. Building your career by nurturing these types of relationships is important.

Building Loyalty in Your Life!

Here are just a few ways and situations in which you can apply my customer loyalty principles:

Land a spouse: Find a good and honest guy or gal and apply these loyalty stages. A successful first date turns a "suspect" into a "prospect" . . . and so forth.

Build a church: Turn a first-time visitor into a loyal member who tithes routinely.

Recruit a new staffer: Vet the applicant and then start the "engagement" process and ultimately turn that new hire into an advocate (raving fan!) that indirectly helps recruit for you.

Grow a donor: Host a party and get potential donors in the room. Turn their first-time donation into repeat donations and, ultimately, advocacy.

Building Loyalty by Stages Is Strategic

What follows is a look at each of those five categories in more detail. And remember, at each stage your goal is to win a "loyal customer." That is, someone who . . .

- Makes regular repeat purchases.
- Purchases across product and service lines.

- Refers others.
- Demonstrates immunity to the pull of the competition.

Contrary to popular opinion, you *can* earn customer loyalty from today's demanding customers. How?

- Look at your in-house capability/system identifying and tracking the four behaviors listed above, customer by customer.
- Look at your customer list and identify which loyalty stage each customer is currently in: suspect, prospect, first-time customer, repeat customer, client, or advocate. (Further on, we'll look at how to win back lost or inactive customers.)
- Create a plan for moving your higher-value customers to the next loyalty stage. If they are already at the advocacy stage, develop a plan for sustaining and leveraging their advocacy.

How to Qualify a Suspect

Does the suspect have . . .

- A problem you can help solve?
- The desire to solve the problem?
- The authority to buy?
- The willingness and ability to pay for your products and services?
- The authority to make a decision within a certain time period?

A yes to all these questions can "graduate" a suspect into a prospect!

Turning Qualified Prospects into First-Time Customers

Bear in mind these realities about moving your new list of qualified prospects to the next stage:

- It takes, on average, seven contacts to turn a prospect into a first-time customer. Research suggests that this "Rule of Seven" is rising (the new number might be closer to ten) because of deeper alliances between buyers and sellers and a tougher economy.
- Customers are attracted to salespeople who listen to their needs, are honest and up front, and diagnose problems and offer solutions.
- It takes patience and time to build trust in a customer. Once trust is gained, there are many long-term benefits.
- Feedback from lost sales reveals valuable information about how to make future sales and build loyalty.

Turning First-Time Customers into Repeat Customers

You've sold someone her first car . . . or computer . . . or Caribbean cruise. Now, how do you guarantee she'll buy a second, third, and fourth time?

Customer Loyalty = Higher Profitability

- Digital marketing offers new and innovative ways to nurture the customer relationship. But to be successful, these new strategies must be built around tried-and-true principles of loyalty.
- A high level of customer satisfaction does not necessarily translate into repeat purchases and increased sales.
- Unlike customer satisfaction, which is geared more toward customer attitude, customer loyalty is behavior based.
- Loyalty is the result of paying attention to what it takes to keep a customer and then constantly providing it as well as upping the value you provide as the relationship matures.
- Increased customer loyalty leads to higher profitability, higher employee retention, and a more stable financial base.

- First-time buyer attrition is often double that of older accounts. Turning the first-time buyer into a repeat customer requires the constant attention of the seller.
- Carefully and continually track the percentage of first-time buyers who become repeat

buyers. Research the reasons first-time customers do not rebuy. Apply what you learn to increase the rate of repeat customers.
- Stay in close touch with frontline employees to identify new and better ways to effectively serve the customer. Hold regular brainstorming meetings with frontline employees to identify recent customer problems and possible ways to address them. Use this information to improve internal processes company wide.

Turning Repeat Customers into Clients

In terms of potential profit payoff, the loyal-client stage is the most critical. To upgrade a repeat customer into a loyal client, a number of actions should be considered. Among them are:

- Underscore the key value your company is known for: operational excellence, customer intimacy, or product leadership. You can accomplish this by: (1) insulating your best customers from competition; (2) making top spenders your first priority; (3) harnessing your supply chain to deliver better customer value; and (4) finding new ways to demonstrate to customers "I know what you need."
- Offer key services to build barriers to the exits and to increase your customers' reluctance

to switch to a competitor.
- Meet regularly with your supply chain partners to identify untapped ways to work together in delivering improved customer value.
- Aggressively seek out ideas from staff about how to better empower employees to serve customers. Continually test new ideas.

Turning Clients into Advocates

At the apex of the successful sales pyramid of satisfied customers sits an advocate of/for your company. What should you do to keep them there?

- Make sure you are ready for new customers! Having advocates refer their friends and acquaintances when you are not ready to deliver only the very best can be a disaster.
- Strive constantly to increase and improve your long-term contacts and indirectly increase your sales. As few as five notes a day, five calls a week, and five meetings a month with your network can give a substantial boost to your business. Remember, the personal touch means a lot in today's high-tech world.

> Stephen Covey: Sharpen the Saw.
>
> A woodcutter strained to saw down a tree. A young man who was watching asked, "What are you doing?"
>
> "Are you blind?" the woodcutter replied. "I'm cutting down this tree."
>
> The young man was unabashed. "You look exhausted! Take a break. Sharpen your saw."
>
> The woodcutter explained to the young man that he had been sawing for hours and did not have time to take a break.
>
> The young man pushed back…. "If you sharpen the saw, you would cut down the tree much faster."
>
> The woodcutter said, "I don't have time to sharpen the saw. Don't you see I'm too busy?"
>
> Lesson: Take time to sharpen your saw. There are endless ways to do it: Attend learning conferences, accept a leadership role in your trade association, send handwritten notes to people you meet.

PART THREE

Life Advice

★ ★ ★

Everybody gets hard knocks, and some of mine came early in life, well before adulthood. Now I see that those early experiences taught me perseverance, self-discipline, and self-preservation. These attributes and skills, in turn, equipped me to blaze my own trail and capitalize on every opportunity, to see them as gifts that might not manifest again.

I also learned one of life's biggest ironies: To serve others well, you have to first care for yourself. Whether that's going to the gym when you would really rather binge-watch Showtime's *Homeland* series or calling it quits when you know you've given your best and you now need downtime. Self care is critical

Coming from a small family, I cultivated the ability early on of how to spot good, decent people that deserved my friendship. I've heard it said, "If you can count on one hand your true friends, you're lucky." That's certainly so in my experience. Life has blessed me with people I've known for better than four decades, in some cases, and they've become family. My minister, Dr. James Mayfield, once told me: "Pay attention to who your friends are, because like it or not, that's what you are becoming." I've found that to be true as well. My friends have held me up in bad times and good, and helped me become the person I am today.

Bottom line: I'm a "glass half-full" gal who sees life as both magical and mysterious. I know in my heart that a guardian angel began watching over me as a child and still is with me today.

Realize What's Truly Important

★ ★ ★

Marsha Griffin Alexander
University of Missouri Extension Specialist, designer, artist

On a very cold January morning in 2003, I was working at my university office. My desk phone rang and it was my doctor's office. The attendant asked me to hold as my doctor wanted to speak with me. A few weeks earlier I had completed my yearly mammogram followed by a recommended biopsy. Over the years I had several biopsies and the results had always been negative. It was no surprise that I would hear directly from my doctor. When he got on the line, however, he said in a stern voice, "Marsha, you have breast cancer. I want you and your husband or another close loved one to visit my office within the next few days so we can discuss the recommended plan of treatment."

At the time I was diagnosed, I was working full-time as a faculty member for a major university. I was also serving as an adjunct assistant professor at a local community college. Each week, the adjunct position required several evenings and some Saturdays in the classroom. As if that wasn't enough, I had begun work on an online PhD program. I was meeting myself coming and going. To say the least, I experienced significant stress on a regular basis.

When my husband and I met with the surgeon, we were both shaken when he told us that in order to ensure the best chance for survival, the recommended strategy was critical. Of course we accepted the physician's advice. Based on his guidance, we met with other physicians and also followed their recommendations. There were two major surgeries involved. Thankfully both were successful and my prognosis was excellent.

My husband and I felt stress had most likely played a role in me getting breast cancer. Out of concern he said, "Marsha, one full-time job should be enough for anyone. You need to get off the crazy marathon and enjoy your life!"

He was right. Shortly after my second surgery I resigned from my adjunct position and I became a PhD dropout! The stress I had just accepted as a given was replaced with more quality time for myself, my family, and my friends. My husband and I particularly enjoyed our time together and pursued many new hobbies, including gardening. Interestingly, the lost income was never missed!!

His guidance that I "stop the crazy marathon and enjoy my life" was indeed the best and wisest advice I have received.

> Not how long, but *how well you have lived* is the main thing.
> —Seneca

Practice Integrity

★ ★ ★

Mel Cooper
CPA, banker, corporate board member

Integrity is the quality of being honest and having strong moral principles, moral uprightness. In the business world, that includes doing deals on a handshake. Shaking hands means you will honor your formal and informal agreements equally. Contracts can be disputed, litigated, and misinterpreted, but if both parties have integrity and are dealing in good faith it, works.

Case in point, some years back I was an executive charged with extending our credit line with a lender group. Our company had been watching our financial results for some time, and we were concerned that we would experience a cash shortfall.

Eventually, I contacted most of the larger lenders in our syndicate because banks would not touch us. All syndicate members except two declined to assist. I moved forward with those two participants on a handshake. Let's call them our "angel lenders." They committed tens of thousands of dollars to help us move forward. We prepared presentations, documentation, and strategy for financing and be-

> Here's a refreshing potpourri of wisdom from iGen/Gen Z thinkers who answered the crowdsourced Internet media company Odyssey's survey, "What Is the Best Piece of Advice You Ever Received?" (December 2017):
>
> Sabrina (18)—The only time to set the bar low is for limbo.
>
> Meg (19)—The secret to success is waking up early.
>
> Caroline (19)—A little love will get you through just about anything. A little kindness from a friend will get you to the next day. A little happiness can keep you going.
>
> Cynthia (19)—*Lo que cuenta es lo de dentro.* (What matters most is what's on the inside.)

gan communicating with other syndicate members.

The business began to improve, along with cash flow and financial outlook, which became considerably more optimistic. Seeing that our business had experienced an upturn, one of the syndicate members that formerly turned me down called to say they would like to lead the refinancing and could certainly offer us better terms than our angel lenders. They were a very well-respected national firm with which almost any company would wish to work.

Sure, they could have handled the transaction by themselves, but that would have left the two original lenders with no stake in the transaction and no return for the time and money they invested to assist our company. I said no. After all, I had a handshake commitment with the angel lenders. We were unable to close a deal with the syndicate because the two angel lenders were unable to reach an agreement with its remaining members. We did find other financing, however, and the company did well.

Two years later one of the angel lenders called and said,

"We didn't get a deal done with you, but we shook hands and you followed through on your commitment. That defines you. I have the right to designate a board member in a public company where I own a significant interest. Would you represent me?"

I said yes.

Time Management

★ ★ ★

Molly Sharpe
Author and community activist

Some of my favorite advice comes from Becca Stevens, founder of Thistle Farms and author. I was fortunate enough to introduce her last year as the speaker for the Eckhardt Mission Series at St. David's Church. When I asked her how she managed to accomplish all she does in a given day, she had two responses. The first was: "We are all busy; we have a choice about what we are busy doing." The second was: "On the road and at home, I do my writing from 5:00 to 8:00 o'clock in the morning before anything else happens."

> In life, you need many more things besides talent. Things like good advice and common sense.
>
> —Hack Wilson
> Baseball Hall of Famer

More Time Management

★ ★ ★

Cheryl Rae
Interactive visualization IT contractor at Balfour and mosaic artist

I really *hate* mowing the lawn. I have allergies and after cutting the grass, I could be sick all day. But someone has to do it, and that someone is always me.

So my dad says, "Map out the route, overlap your circles a little bit so you don't have to go back and do it again, and it will take you so much less time." He was teaching me how to mow correctly and efficiently, but I recognized he was teaching me something more important and long lasting. If there is something you hate doing, concentrate on the most efficient process to get it done so you'll be done faster and can get on with the better stuff of life.

One day my tenant came out while I was mowing the lawn and offered to do it. He gave me a cream soda to sit down and enjoy while he mowed. Well, he didn't know the circles plan and must have gone around that teeny yard twenty-five times! (It takes me four swipes in concentric circles.) Waste of time, gas, and my patience!! Plus he was leaving these standing sprigs everywhere. I was antsy for him to understand this was something that had to be done, so let's get it over with. I've never given up the handle on my mower again.

> The best advice I ever received is that there is a difference between urgency and importance: Urgent tasks seem important, but they're not. Important things need to get done.
>
> —Chieh Huang
> CEO, Boxed.com

Never Stop Believing

★ ★ ★

John Hallman
CEO Hallman Group

The best advice came from my mom when I had quit high school with no job. I moved to Charlotte to a one-room dump and was taking university-level courses at UNCC and working full-time.

I called her one night in tears saying, "I can't do this!" to which she said, "Yes you can, and don't stop believing!" I struggled on and graduated with honors, then went on to get my MBA. The rest is history.

I got in the computer business in 1984 just when Microsoft and others were coming along. I got lucky and bought a few shares and was on my way.

My dad also gave me great advice when he said, "Never forget where you came from, and work hard."

The most meaningful elements in my success were my education and that "never stop believing" attitude, which enhanced my life by allowing me to be able to help others and see the world. When you believe in yourself it creates all kinds of positive vibes!

(Note: The money part is nice, of course, but not the most important!)

> It's common for people to start questioning themselves. As a female, I'm going to offer the advice I gave myself: You look at your strengths, you look at your goals, and accept that you are who you are. Be true to that.
>
> —Joy Mangano
> President, Ingenious Designs, LLC

FOLLOW THESE LEADERS

Bring Your Big Heart

★ ★ ★

John Pincelli
Real estate attorney

With our busy lives we meet scores and scores of people. Everybody deserves respect. But, does everybody deserve your help? The only advice I can give with a high degree of confidence is, don't ever help anybody with the expectation of getting something back. If you do that, you're not helping, you're battering. Just show on up with your big old heart.

> One piece of advice that stuck in my mind is that people should be respected and trusted as people, not because of their position or title.
>
> —Herb Kelleher
> Cofounder, Chairman Emeritus, former CEO,
> Southwest Airlines

Keep It Simple

★ ★ ★

Imogen Coe
Dean of Faculty of Science, and Professor of Biology, Ryerson University

My great mentor, Dr. Gillian Wu, who was the Dean of Science at York University for a while when I was a faculty member in biology there, once gave me solid advice about parenting when I was struggling as a single mother of two small children as a consequence of having my partner removed from the house for abuse. "Keep 'em alive, just keep 'em alive," she said. It was the same advice she gave my colleague and friend who was struggling with divorce and whose teenagers were going off the rails.

Dr. Wu had been widowed young, leaving her with two young boys, so she knew a thing or two. For me, her advice meant just focus on the core things: Keep the kids alive and don't sweat the other stuff. Keep them fed and housed and loved. That's it. Everything else is gravy. Don't stress about it. It helped me at a time when all I could really do was get through the day and then the next day and . . . I was keeping them alive! It's the best parenting advice ever and just about the only advice I've ever considered worth paying attention to!

> Never do for a child what he is capable of doing for himself.
>
> —Elizabeth Hainstock

Wait Three Days

★ ★ ★

Stephanie Salb
Family law practitioner

The majority of issues in our lives really do not require immediate attention, although we may think that they do at the time. When the path is unclear, and particularly when I do not feel at peace about a matter that demands action, I use the "three-day rule." I am not sure to whom I owe credit for this wise concept that I heard years ago.

Three days . . . quite a bit can happen in this relatively short window of time. The old song "What a Difference a Day Makes" captures the sentiment of wait and see. Three days (or 72 hours or 4,320 minutes) is an appreciable length of time

> According to *Business Insider*'s Richard Feloni, Arianna Huffington, president and editor-in-chief of The Huffington Post Media Group, always got the same advice from her mother when she felt hopeless. Her mom likened facing adversity to watching a horror film on TV: "Darling, just change the channel. You are in control of the clicker. Don't replay the bad, scary movie."

in which not only to weigh options but also to assess developments. Twenty-four hours can be too brief, while a week can be too long a delay.

When I am faced with a decision in which there are no easy answers or obvious options, I simply wait three days in which to pray and ponder and watch. Often, the answer is apparent by then. At other times, a decision may not be imminent but a path is emerging as events occur and more information is available. Either way, I cannot think of a time when I regretted waiting three days.

Short, Sweet, Powerful

★ ★ ★

Tom Stacy
Founding Partner, CapRidge Partners LLC

The advice I was given several decades ago that I have come to believe with all my heart and soul was in a sermon by my best friend and mentor, Dr. Ralph Smith, pastor of Hyde Park Baptist Church in Austin, Texas.

- Things are not as bad as they seem.
- Things could be worse.
- Things will get better.

> I have dedicated decades of my life in the elected public service arena to make a positive difference. My mom and dad taught me from a very early age: "It's not the dollars you make, it's the difference you make!"
>
> — Carole Keeton
> Former Texas comptroller of public accounts and former mayor of Austin, Texas

Try a New Perspective

★ ★ ★

Karen Hargett

Cardiovascular Technologist (Retired)

My parents taught [my brother and me] the importance of "walking away" when the project or problem wasn't easily solved. Returning to that project fifteen to thirty minutes later with a fresh mind and perspective gave them the ability to see what they had missed earlier.

A stellar example of this was when we were studying the definition of a preposition in grade school. I couldn't get "a word that governs a noun or pronoun and expresses a relation to other words in a sentence."

After a couple of nights of listening to me struggle, Dad said he really wanted me to understand the definition but in the meantime to step away from the textbook and think, "A squirrel goes up a tree, around a tree, between trees." Wow! Talk about a lightbulb moment!

Look the Part

★ ★ ★

John Maxwell
Retired Texas State Trooper

When our youngest was fourteen he was in a program called Sea Cadets, a paramilitary organization for kids sponsored by the Navy League. One of their service projects was to assist with parking and providing labor during the Texas Parks and Wildlife Department's annual fall fair/expo.

He dressed up in the prescribed outfit—camo uniform and combat boots—and I drove him to the fair site, which was awash in people. To find his duty station I told him to get out of the car and ask one of the men working an information booth where to go. He got out of the car, braced himself, and approached the booth. All of the people surrounding it parted to create a path for him to the head of the line. When he stepped forward, all three men working the booth stopped what they were doing and turned to help him. He received the directions he needed and came back to the car.

I asked him if he saw what had happened. He looked puzzled and said no. I pointed out that he was the youngest person out of the twenty or so people at that booth. He agreed that was probably right. Then I pointed out how all of the people waiting had stepped aside to allow him to go ahead of them and how the men in the booth had all stopped to help him before going on to help the others. He looked puzzled again and wondered why that happened.

I explained it wasn't because of who he was, what he knew, or what he wanted that mattered. I asked him if he thought the way he was dressed mattered. You could see the light dawn in his eyes. I asked him if he thought a sloppy-looking person would have received the same treatment. He didn't think so. There was more conversation about how he carried himself, how he used "Yes sir" and "No sir" and "Please." The best part was, I never again had to ask the questions you face with most teenage boys: Did you bathe? Are those clothes clean? Have you shined your shoes? He got what mattered

> When I was fourteen, a guy friend of mind complimented my shirt. I immediately deflected the compliment by assuring him it wasn't *that* expensive and was an old shirt.
>
> He looked right at me and said: "If you make giving you a compliment a chore, people will stop giving them. Just say thank you."
>
> From that moment on, whenever I get a compliment, I look the person in the eyes and say, "Thank you so much."
> —L. C. Mills, psychology undergrad major, University of Victoria

Practice Insane Courage

★ ★ ★

Melinda Garvey
Founder and Publisher, AW Media, Inc., and 2011–2012 Entrepreneur in Residence for The McCombs School of Business at the University of Texas at Austin

One piece of great advice that sticks with me actually comes from the movie *We Bought a Zoo*. Matt Damon says to his son: "Sometimes, all you need is twenty seconds of insane courage . . . just literally twenty seconds of embarrassing bravery and I promise you, something great will come of it."

If we all could live by this every day—especially women—just think about how our lives would be transformed, and how we might transform the lives of others. Twenty seconds of courage feels easily attainable, so we will push ourselves to do it without even considering that so much impact can be made in that short amount of time.

You'll Never Go Wrong

★ ★ ★

Barbara Hendricks
Celebrated Book Publicist

Leadership guru John C. Maxwell gave me this advice: There is no need to create a separate set of "rules" for business—bring the same character, ethics, and values that guide your personal life. You'll never go wrong.

> My life is my message.
> —Mahatma Gandhi

Own Your Life

★ ★ ★

Lucas Miller
Founder and CEO, Echelon Copy

The best business advice I ever received came from John Warrillow's *Built to Sell* [subtitled *Creating a Business That Can Thrive Without You*]. More than a piece of advice, the book gave me a new outlook on owning my own business: Entrepreneurship is about building a lifestyle for yourself, not just another nine-to-five job in which you're your own boss.

Before reading this book, I was a bit of a one-man-band, so to speak. Now, instead of trying to do everything myself, I work with people who possess skills I simply don't have. I'm able to tap into their expertise to give myself time to live my life while also building a worthwhile career.

Yes, just like every other entrepreneur, I live a life loaded with things that cause stress, but the stress is much more manageable than it used to be.

Thanks to expanding my team, I'm able to work without actually being at the office. I'm not perfect at this by any means, but I've already gotten a solid taste of where I can adjust my situations to fit the needs of the moment. I love it.

Cash In on Social Capital

★ ★ ★

Patti DeNucci
Founder and CEO, DeNucci & Co. LLC and Rosewall Press

I've been blessed with dozens of mentors and guides over the years and they've taught me many lessons that I apply in both business and life. But one lesson stands out as the foundation for just about everything I do. It's from my paternal grandfather, Howard Allen (H.A.) Parks.

Back in the 1930s Grampa H.A. was an entrepreneur struggling to keep his Chevrolet auto dealership afloat in Chisholm, a small, remote town on the Iron Range of Northern Minnesota. Cars were emerging as a new way to get around, but the Great Depression was in full swing and many people were out of work and struggling financially, so owning a newfangled, high-luxury item like a car was simply out of the question. To top that off, General Motors was manufacturing very few new cars during that time because demand had dropped so significantly.

Grampa had no inventory to sell except for one used car he had purchased from a customer who could no longer afford to keep it. (That's the kind of person Grampa was; always trying to help others out, even amid his own

> My Nana said to me: "Carol, at the end of every day, you should ask yourself two questions. What did I learn today? What did I do to make a difference?" For the longest time, I chased the big opportunity and juggled multimillion-dollar potential sales. Now I no longer chase dollar signs but river polluters, and search not for the next big opportunity but for ripples and rapids and more of nature's music.
> —Carol Parenzan, Middle Susquehanna Riverkeeper

challenges.) But he did have some very powerful friends in his corner, including the bank president. Knowing how hard Grampa worked and how much ingenuity he had, his banker friend pulled a few strings that allowed Grampa to delay one or two monthly payments for the building that housed the dealership as well as the apartment where Grampa and Gramma lived.

The economic issues of the day weren't going to go away quickly, and the grace period offered by the banker couldn't last forever. Things were pretty bleak.

And then they got bleaker. Grampa had to produce a payment by the end of day on a certain Friday or the bank would have no choice but to foreclose. He wasn't happy about this, but he didn't complain. He did the only thing he could think of: He sprang into action.

He had plenty of social capital. It was time to cash in on it.

Grampa made a lot of stops the Thursday before the deadline: He popped into every café, grocery store, bakery, post office, and watering hole he could think of. And not just in Chisholm, but all across the Iron Range. He told the people he ran into what he was trying to do and what was at stake. Because of their love, admiration, and respect for Grampa, people did what they could to help. Some could only give him encouragement and a cup of hot coffee, but others were able to offer leads and ideas on where to go next in search of a buyer for the car.

One of those leads sounded promising. Word had it that a fireman in a nearby town had been able to save some money and was interested in a car. Grampa headed in that direction and found the man on duty at the fire station. He took the man for a test drive, offered to sell the car to the man at a fair price, and the man accepted. What's more, the fireman was able to pay Grampa in cash, buy him a celebratory beer, and give him a ride back home in time for supper.

Grampa strode into the bank the next morning and put the cash on his friend's desk. The business was saved!

My sisters and I each worked for Dad (in the car dealership!) during our high school and college years and learned valuable lessons about running a business: How to treat people, earn and keep solid reputations as citizens, and be responsible and visionary leaders in the community.

Those lessons form the basis for the work I do now, teaching people about the importance of attracting, growing, and benefiting from meaningful business connections.

One person I told H.A.'s story to remarked that it was like something out of a Frank Capra movie. I would have to agree. It was a pivotal time in the history of my family and is a testimony to the value of being good to all people, every day, so that one day, when you need help, they will be willing and happy to return the favor.

Mission Field or Battlefield?

★ ★ ★

Bill Fitzpatrick
Cofounder and Senior VP of Sales & Marketing at
3b2 Solutions

The Presbyterian minister walked slowly to the lectern and began his sermon, just as he had done for so many years. Reverend Al was not one to use a lot of fancy words, nor was he the type to view just one side of an issue. I liked that about him. He always saw both sides of the coin.

On that particular Sunday in 1993, he spoke about the importance of applying biblical lessons to our outside-of-church, Monday-to-Saturday world. If you are in business, he offered, perhaps you should view the workplace and your customers as a Christian mission field and less as a battlefield in which to make a profit. Were his words surprising? No. Have others offered the same lines of thought? Yes. Did his words change the way I came to view my approach to business? Absolutely.

In both of the companies I have led, I am ever mindful of Reverend Al's message. I do not always get it right, that's for sure, but my job is to be patient with employees, meet them "where they are," and help them achieve their professional goals. My approach with our customers, some of whom are the largest restaurant companies in the world, is to listen to their needs, to help solve their problems, to become an extension of their Information Technology staff, to earn their trust. On several occasions I have taken calls from the companies we service asking us to just get this major project done, and they know we will charge them "a fair price" at the end of the day. These large companies could have called IBM, NCR, or HP, but they called us instead.

I no longer attend that church, but I still drive past it on a regular basis. Yup, the sign is still there that Reverend Al had planted twenty-five years ago. The words on the sign can be read only as you leave the parking lot. They say, "You are now entering the mission field."

To be sure, I have received plenty of academic wisdom, and a few people along the way have shared some helpful advice in what it takes to make an informed decision or how best to grow a company. But for me, I know I am best at applying the business lessons that anyone can, in truth, learn by overlaying those with my religious beliefs. It is not always easy and I often miss the mark, but I try. And, thankfully, we are very profitable.

Thanks, Dad

★ ★ ★

Tracy Prager Schell
Project Lead, 183S Project Highway system

Short and sweet, but it's served me well. From my father, Jerome L. Prager: "Be yourself and people will flock to you."

> To think well and to consent to obey someone giving good advice are the same thing.
>
> —Herodotus
> Greek historian, 5th century BC

Honesty and Integrity Are Not for Sale

★ ★ ★

Kathy Taylor
Civic leader and philanthropist

When I was a young woman, in the course of shopping for a new outfit, I started a conversation with the salesgirl helping me, who was probably close to my age at the time. I was telling her that I really liked two different outfits, but I could only afford to buy one of them and was trying to decide which one I would buy. She told me that she could place both in the shopping bag while I paid for only one of them.

She then said, "No one will ever know."

Well, I would know!

I was so startled by her suggestion that it took a minute to answer her. I was raised in a Christian home and taught that honesty and integrity, without question, were essential qualities for every member of our family. Since my income at the time was very meager, this was admittedly a bit of a temptation, if only briefly. I told the girl that I couldn't do that and left with my one outfit paid in full. I have never forgotten that experience and how it made me feel about myself.

No position, recognition, or pay raise is worth sacrificing your honor and integrity for. I'm thankful for what my parents taught me, since those values are what I strive to always carry with me into all settings and aspects of life.

> What is left when honor is lost?
>
> —Publilius Syrus, first century BC

Leaving Home

★ ★ ★

Janet Barry Mullins
Certified Registered Nurse Anesthetist

The most memorable parenting advice I ever received was from my father as I was pulling out of the driveway on my way to start my new life in Charleston, South Carolina.

"Remember these three things," he said.

- "You can always come home, always.
- Change your oil every three thousand miles.
- And NEVER do business with people with a fish by their name."

I promptly moved across the street from the "Christian" Exxon station proprietor who ripped me off repeatedly!!! The last time I ever did business with him, he said, "I have changed your oil, rotated your tires, and checked out your rear end."

I innocently said, "Thank you."

He replied, "I checked out your rear end as you walked

> The most useful piece of advice I've gotten for both business and personal situations is from my mom and dad. They taught me from the time I was a little girl to follow my heart and pursue my dreams. Because if you follow your heart and truly pursue your dreams, you will never really feel that you have worked a day in your life.
> —Lexi Thompson, LPGA, 2014 ANA Inspiration tournament winner

all the way back to your apartment."(Wish we'd had the #MeToo movement back then!)

My dad also gave me very solid advice when it came to pursuing my life ambition. "Never close a door, and if it closes but it's something you want, beat on it 'til it opens. Go after anything you really want." Of all the character traits a human can possess, perseverance is the most important. More important than brains and looks and money.

My mother's advice that has really stuck with me is, "If you don't point out your flaws, no one else will notice them." Oh, and "Always be kind."

Don't Get Stuck in the Middle

★ ★ ★

Bruce Kasanoff
Cofounder, Ikigai Park City, and coauthor of *I Am*

One of my professors from Wharton, Ken Smith, taught me an incredibly valuable lesson. He argued that everyone perceives himself or herself to be stuck in the middle. Middle managers feel stuck in the middle, yes, but CEOs feel stuck between employees and the board, investors, and analysts. Star actors feel stuck between the studios, directors, and audience expectations. It goes on and on. You will always feel stuck in the middle UNTIL you realize you have a much greater ability to control your fate than you think. You just have to be willing to pay the price—that is, risk, uncertainty, upheaval, etc.—of that change. You

> Well, my dad always tells me to not spend, and [instead] to save, because you never know what's going to happen in the future. Know what you're spending, know what you're saving. Don't spend it all at once.
> —Michelle Wie, LPGA, 2014 U.S. Women's Open winner

won't have power when you get the big job; you'll have power when you take responsibility for change.

> Your level of success is determined by your level of discipline and perseverance.
>
> —Anonymous

Recognize Your Blessings

★ ★ ★

Arie Brish
President, cxo360

My mother taught me this important lesson: No matter how bad the situation is, it can be worse. She spent her teenage years in a Nazi concentration camp in World War II. Her motto was to feel sorry for those that suffered more than her. If she had one slice of bread for the week, she felt sorry for those who didn't get to eat at all. I took that advice to heart and try to always look for the opportunity in bad situations.

Work Behind the Scenes

★ ★ ★

Adam Quinton
Founder and CEO of Lucas Point Ventures, adjunct professor, Columbia University, School of International and Public Affairs

A dear uncle of mine passed away last year. I went back to the UK for a touching remembrance ceremony for him where family, friends, and colleagues shared their memories of him. He was a senior academic and often had a hand in selecting or advising various universities on appointments in his field. What was very touching was the number of female colleagues who went to the microphone and explained how he had helped their careers along, had intervened on their behalf at key moments—and yet they never knew, at the time, he had done it. And he never sought credit or praise afterwards.

Two key points from that I think:

> 1. What really matters when you champion or sponsor a person is not what you say when they are in the room. It is what you say when they are NOT in the room and when you put your own name at risk.

2. I had absolutely no idea about this side of my uncle. But he had clearly followed the Dr. Cornel West philosophy. He was just a good guy trying to do the right thing. So hopefully I can be a little like him myself.

> There is no limit to the amount of good you can do if you don't care who gets the credit.
>
> —Ronald Reagan

Managing Highs and Lows

★ ★ ★

Adam J. Epstein
Third Creek Advisors, LLC

My father, Ira Epstein, told me when I was a kid: "There are many things that change with time, but great entrepreneurs will always have three key attributes: they don't get too high on the 'highs' or too low on the 'lows,' they remain humble, and they are always constructively paranoid about everything they've built disappearing in the blink of an eye."

Though my father unfortunately passed away many years ago, his words only ring truer with the inexorable passage of time.

Dress for Success

★ ★ ★

Jill Griffin
Recreational Shopper

First impressions count! Whether you are about to interview for a new job, are making a big presentation, or going to an important gathering, wearing a blazer (or jacket, for the ladies) broadcasts some worthy messages:

> "I've got my act together," "I'm serious," "You matter and I'm putting my best foot forward." "I'm invested in myself and I mean business."

> Do you have an important meeting on the horizon? If so, pull out that blazer from the back of your closet or go buy one!

> Know this: The blazer is timeless. (It's as powerful—and popular—in today's business world as it was in the twentieth century!) Don't blow your chance at making a great first impression.

Stay One Step Ahead

★ ★ ★

Jane Frances C. Gentapanan
Recruitment specialist

Always be one step ahead of your clients, and always be one step ahead of your candidates.

This is a great piece of advice from my first mentor in recruitment, Mr. Sajid Hussein, former General Manager of Talent Management Consultancy for almost twenty years. Experience is indeed the best teacher, and you are even luckier when you learn from people with experience.

The reality in a recruiter's role is that life is filled with ups and downs and turnarounds. I was a newbie in recruitment nine years ago when I was with Talent, and I clearly remember my first successful placement. It did not come easily and there was lack of clarity at several points along the way. Sometimes you will have good clients and candidates, and sometimes they will be less than stellar. Bearing this piece of advice in mind and putting it into practice, I ensure effective communication to build good relationships with my clients and candidates, from the beginning to a successful placement.

Effective communication with clients requires timing

and rapport; knowing when to follow up; and what to say and ask so you can gauge the possibilities of your success. You should be able to gain information to help you in your next course of action.

Effective communication with the candidates, on the other hand, will keep you in the loop of where they stand on the opportunity you found them with your clients. Successful placement can be a quick or a lengthy process. At times, a candidate may lose interest, entertain another opportunity, withdraw the application, or reject the offer. If you establish a good relationship with them through providing feedback in a timely manner, or even just giving them a ring to let them know the job is still active, you can anticipate roadblocks to a successful placement.

This piece of advice from my mentor gives me a broader perspective and understanding why it is so important to always establish good communication with both clients and candidates.

Pay Attention

★ ★ ★

Leisa Holland-Nelson
Vice President/CMO, ASTOUNDZ

"The customer is your business and not an interruption," Stanley Marcus said. It may be the best advice ever, especially for someone just starting out. We all get frustrated with our clients—and children, friends, loved ones—but when we remember that we would be out of business without them it really changes our attitude for the better and allows us to open up, learn, be gracious, and be our best selves!

In another piece of advice that sounds simple but really requires training and attention, Gene Rappoport, EVP, Federated Department Stores, and founder, Federated Merchandising Services, said, "Listen." Great leaders listen and recognize that people often tell you what they want. This is my skill I am most proud of and would absolutely never have gotten it without the guidance and unrelenting pushing from Gene! I heard "shut up and listen" more times than I want to remember. We young geniuses know it all!!! Right?

Passion to Serve

★ ★ ★

Miranda Coutee
Seventh Grade English Language Arts teacher,
Intrinsic Schools

The best business advice I've ever received was from my dad. When I graduated from college and began to schedule interviews with schools, he told me not to focus on salary/money, but instead to find what I was passionate about and everything else would fall into place. He also said that what you do for a living is not who you are, but whatever you do, be sure that you are serving others, as that should be your purpose. In two short years in the workforce, I've sincerely benefitted from his direction. It is a pleasure to wake up each day and look forward to enhancing my students' lives and hopefully encouraging them to find their own passion and purpose in life.

JILL GRIFFIN

Don't Undercut Your Value

★ ★ ★

Sean Barber
CEO, Poly-Mart Inc.

Sometimes the best business lessons find you when you least want them, but their importance supersedes the bad timing.

I was twenty-two years old and under immense pressure building a start-up factory. I had high fixed-costs, a workforce that hadn't been taught their specific skill set yet, and I was dealing with constant manufacturing problems (utility issues, permitting, and such) that had nothing to do with the core business.

I had secured a much-needed new customer who wanted yellow trash dumpsters made. Up until that point, I had manufactured the more standard colors of commercial dumpsters such as green, blue, and black. Despite the molds being cleaned, a chemical reaction was occurring between the yellow and previous colors used in them. A green film was evident on the yellow dumpsters. Having absolutely no margin for error to afford any rejects, and knowing that the dumpsters were still fit for their intended use, I tried to fix the aesthetic blemish.

As a few of us were fervently scrubbing the dumpsters to remove as much green film as possible, my father walked into the factory for an unscheduled visit. He is successful and the hardest worker I've ever known. Growing up, I rarely witnessed others match his frankness. He saw me stressed and disheveled and asked me what I was doing. In the Phoenix heat he patiently heard me out, then asked in a reprimanding voice: "What kind of message are you sending by letting product like that leave? That's not how you build or sustain a successful company!"

Considering the circumstances and my exhaustion, I was not in the best frame of mind. Yet in that moment, the fog lifted. I realized he was right, and without my explicitly knowing it, my culture of quality was born.

One of the ways my company is different from others was customization in color and assembly, yet here I was undercutting that value. It takes years of work and constant sowing to build an internal company culture. That culture gets reinforced or diminished on every order. We ultimately decide in which direction the needle moves every day.

I realized at that moment that customers purchase solutions, not problems. I was cutting a corner and by doing so sending the wrong message not only to the market but also to my employees who I entrust to take care of the customer. I was not leading by example. In my company now, this quality buy-in affects all parts of the business, from customer service to operations to the supply chain. It is part of our identity. We don't look at our products as just a dollar value but an extension of who we are and what we as a manufacturer deliver for our clients. This focus on quality and the outside view of the customer has resulted in success for the business.

I think about that hot summer day a lot, especially when I proudly see our products at businesses and homes. I was too busy watching the few dollars I had instead of looking at the longer strategic window we should be building. I owe that lesson to the last and only time as an adult I was scolded by my dad. Good lessons don't care how old you are. You know the truth when it's spoken to you.

> There are plenty of things I wish I'd known when I decided to quit my position at IBM and work on the idea that later became TaskRabbit. Maybe that's why one of the things I cherish most about being a founder and CEO is the opportunity to offer advice to new entrepreneurs.
>
> —Leah Busque
> General Partner, Fuel Capital

One Simple Rule

★ ★ ★

Carey Leva
Senior Vice President, Wealth Advisor, and Trust Officer, Broadway Bank

This sounds really elementary, but years ago when I was a young attorney, one of my mentors told me: "Always try to return phone calls or emails the same day. If you can't do that, at least within twenty-four hours. If you can't do that, have your assistant contact them and let them know you are busy but will respond by a certain time." That is some of the best advice I ever got!

Treat Everyone Well

★ ★ ★

Fred J. Silhanek
Senior Vice President, Development, Luby's Fuddruckers Restaurants, LLC

Early in my career with Pepperidge Farm Bakeries, my branch manager and I were making my first visit to a grocery store. He said, "Treat everyone working at the store with respect and dignity; The person mopping the floors today may be the General Manager you need to deal with tomorrow."

Be Genuine

★ ★ ★

Kristen James
Social Media strategist

A mentor and good friend once told me that those who are their true selves, no matter the situation, will make stronger connections and live happier lives.

It seems so straightforward, but in many cases, we may find ourselves putting on an act to impress someone or performing in the way we think others want to engage with us. As a people-pleaser to my core, I've fallen prey to this habit many times, especially when I found myself in situations where I was either the youngest or the least experienced in the room. To combat this pattern, I've worked over the last few years to engage more genuinely with my coworkers, friends, and even my mother-in-law! As my mentor suggested, this has led to creating stronger friendships and more impactful business relationships because the connection is real.

The more genuine I am with others, the more likely they are to open up with me as well, creating stronger and more authentic bonds.

> I think it's important for whatever you are doing . . . to seek outside advice. If your world becomes too insular, it limits your creativity.
> —Georgina Chapman
> Cofounder, Marchesa fashion label

There Is No Big "C"

★ ★ ★

NeCall Wilson
Certified Career Coach

There is no big "C"! Treat *all* your customers well.

I heard this advice from the IBM New Hire Training Manager [back in] 1991. It has enhanced my life continuously because it has proven to be so true. Whether servicing a $200 client or a $4 billion client—premier customer service is a must.

Develop a great brand of servant leadership and then demonstrate it daily. I have made an effort to be the best service provider for all my clients with no regard to their contribution to the bottom line.

Great customer service should be just that: great customer service for all. That advice has served me well in and out of the office. It is now part of who I am. (Thanks, Big Blue.)

Watch, Wait, and Listen

★ ★ ★

Randy Brandt

Adjunct Professor of Communications, Xavier University

I've had many great teachers, but one of the best was the late Harvey Penick, legendary golf pro and teacher of life's lessons. I don't always succeed in putting it into practice, but I try to keep the following advice close to heart: "Criticize yourself once in a while instead of others, and see what you might be doing wrong. Speak ill of no one, and all the good you know of everyone. Don't judge a person too soon. God waits until the end."

Where I Hope This Book Takes You

Humans have a huge appetite (what we Southerners call "a hankerin'") for seeking advice on just about any subject you can imagine—be it etiquette, home remedies like those in *The Farmers' Almanac*, quick fixes to repair broken objects, or be it tips on how to negotiate a raise (or to raise children), to handle office rivals, or to invest our money. We want to become more adaptable and to be ready for whatever life throws at us in terms of relationships and hardships.

I began to collect and review contributors' stories for this book, I discovered that many of them dealt with familiar situations, yet their fresh answers and hard-earned advice taught me so much!

Among the big lessons I learned?

1. People are kind, generous, and happy to share

their advice. All you have to do is simply ask.

2. Wisdom is everywhere. Start a search of your own, perhaps, simply by typing into a search box a topic you are curious about. Shazam! Deep learning is there for the curious and courageous.

3. Always be learning! There's a big world out there awaiting your talents. Strive to be all you can be.

It's my sincere hope that this collection of advice from the fields, the classrooms, the mountaintops, and the C-Suites will fall softly upon you and sink into your minds. And I trust you'll listen to its music "profoundly," letting it flower and grow in your own lives and, when appropriate, pass it along.

I close with an "ask." In this book, you have read a lot of advice, from many sources. No doubt, some are your favorites and others not. Would you email me which stories you liked and why? That way the next edition can be "spot-on" for you! You can reach me at jillgriffin1@icloud.net.

Thank you for being on this reading journey with me!
Jill

FOLLOW THESE LEADERS

More...

Tissa Richards is founder and CEO of Network Kinetix, a company based in Austin, Texas, that helps enterprises protect their reputations and revenues from network threats. She has worked with a combination of F500 and start-ups in Silicon Valley for her entire career and brings a unique—and honest—perspective to what it really means to put your life savings and energy into launching a company.

She graciously offered the following material to help interested readers of *Follow These Leaders* determine where they are on the spectrum of readiness to dive into the pool labeled "ready to launch my start-up."

ARE YOU READY TO START A COMPANY?

You may be familiar with the oft-quoted statistic that 90 percent of start-ups fail. However, that may not actually be true. Cambridge Associates tracked 27,000+ VC-backed start-ups and found that the failure rate has not risen above 60 percent since 2001. (Failure was defined as companies that provide a 1x or lower return to investors.) So, put that far less onerous statistic into your head: 60 percent of companies fail, not 90 percent. Which means your actual odds of success are ~4x higher than conventional wisdom would have you believe.

Despite that more appealing statistic, most start-up stories do not have the glamour of the well-known success stories like Facebook and Mark Zuckerberg. I want to share some blunt truths from the trenches. What follows are some very real and probing questions you should ask yourself before you jump into launching a company. These questions should make you think about the effect this decision will have on your personal life and your finances; about your true (not your desired) personality and work type; and your ability to roll with the very real punches that the start-up life will throw at you on a minute-to-minute basis. Sanity-check yourself on the honesty of your answers to these questions. If you can't honestly answer yes to most of these questions, there may be other paths you are better suited for.

Are you prepared for the financial sacrifice?

Do you have the personal savings to finance your company for an undetermined time until you can raise outside funding or build it to a comfortable profit level? Whatever you think that timeline to funding or profitability will be . . . double it.

Can you absorb the opportunity cost of going without an income for that same time period (and most likely, beyond it)? Most early investment rounds will not include a salary for the founder/CEO. Can you handle the double-whammy of putting your life savings into the company and foregoing a salary? This is a key reality to be prepared for.

There is a third hidden cost here: Your friends and peer group will not be making this same sacrifice. They will keep doing whatever it is they do, and what you've been accustomed to doing with them—going to dinners, out to bars, or weekends away. It will get harder and harder to do this with them, and that will become progressively more difficult to experience and to sacrifice.

Are you prepared for the emotional toll?

You will experience the highest highs and the lowest lows in the same day. There are days you will experience them in the same hour. Sometimes, you'll experience them in a single meeting. This is more akin to emotional whiplash than to an emotional rollercoaster. You have to learn to keep your head up and keep your cool. This will take a toll on you and it will take a secondary toll on the people in your life.

You will be tired from this, and it will burn you out. Make sure there are things in your life that will counterbalance the burnout. Do you have mentors, family, or friends who are willing to lift your spirits when you need it? Do you have hobbies and activities that recharge and reenergize you? Remember, you won't have a lot of spare time. Are these things that you can access in short bursts that will still feed your soul?

Are you prepared to work painfully long hours, weekends & holidays (basically, always)?

You will not have a "normal" work schedule until you exit the company. You frequently won't even be aware of how many hours you are putting in because you will be (should be) doing something you love that will, in fact, energize you. But be aware that it will eat into the time you would otherwise be doing non-work things.

I frequently schedule meetings on statutory holidays because I truly don't distinguish between holidays and a "regular" working day. It isn't until recipients decline meeting requests with bemused responses that I become aware that the rest of the world isn't working on that day. Retirees say they don't know what day it is because every day feels like a weekend. The startup world is the inverse: Every day feels like a workday. At times, I'd rather have the "retiree's dilemma"!

Are you prepared for the loneliness?

This will be one of the most intensely lonely and private experiences of your life. You will also simultaneously be awash with advice from and interactions with a lot of people. You'll have to decide how to balance the two. The key takeaway from this is that you'll have to keep a lot of things to yourself while presenting a consistently positive face to the world. It's a long and frequently stressful road, yet you can't let it show.

Make sure you have a support network discrete from your company. You'll need them to listen to you and hold you up. Your neck will get tired as you hold your head up high no matter how much weight is on your shoulders. Make sure this support network is comprised of people you trust. Ideally, these will be people who understand enough about what you are doing to be empathetic, but distant enough not to be involved in the minutiae. You will want and need that distance.

Do you need immediate gratification?

Are you able to stay focused while working extremely hard for a long time on something where the fruits of your labor may not be readily apparent (or recognized) for months, or even years? You will need to develop and hone the skill of identifying and celebrating small victories and progress. If identifying these is difficult for you, it may prove to be frustrating. Think of it like training for the Olympics. Are you prepared for all the discipline, competitions, injuries, sacrifices, and emotional setbacks it takes to reach that medal podium years in the future?

Are you persuasive?

Can you convince others to see what you see? You will need to bring a wide variety of other people along on this journey with you. In some ways, you'll have to project the charisma of a cult leader and persuade your team and your early adopters to drink the Kool-Aid. Your vision of the product, the value proposition, and the market value have to be incredibly compelling. You have to persuade people to pitch in (hopefully for free), for equity, or for far below market rates.

At one point, we had nearly 20 people working with or advising the company with a combined ~375 years of experience. If all of those people were compensated, we would have been looking at well over $6M a year. Instead, we were able to keep our burn rate significantly lower for a long time. Combined with equity grants, I managed to be passionate, persuasive, and compelling enough to bring a lot of those extremely experienced and valuable advisors along on the journey without it costing the company market rates.

Are you articulate?

This is partly a follow-on to the persuasiveness question above. Can you explain what you are doing and why? You don't have to be your own marketing guru. In fact, you need to clearly recognize where your strengths and weaknesses lie. You may not be the best person to finalize your messaging and create your marketing collateral. But something is propelling you to take this crazy leap from ideation to commercialization. Can you passionately articulate it? If you can't, it will be a harder struggle.

Can you handle conflict?

Are you comfortable being assertive and handling the inevitable and frequent situations that will require you to navigate conflict? From Day 1, you will have to be unapologetic about your value and credibility—even when it hasn't yet been proven in the marketplace or with customers. This gets easier with time, but if this is something you instinctively flinch from, think hard about whether this is the right path for you. You will have to fire people, negotiate, and defend your pricing, your valuation, and your decisions. You can learn to take the combat out of conflict, but if you can't take the anxiety out of it, this may always be a weak spot for you.

In my company's first quarter of operation, two vendors went to war with each other. I was not experienced at handling conflict at the time and dreaded having to mediate. I had to psych myself up for those calls in a major way and my discomfort was transparent. Now I can handle those types of calls while at the grocery store, with zero preparation. It has become par for the course as I've learned to comfortably remove the emotion from the conflict.

Can you admit when you need advice & mentorship?

The underlying question here is: Do you know your strengths and weaknesses, and are you willing to articulate them to your advisors and mentors?

Being extremely honest with yourself about what you are good at and where your skills are lacking will accelerate your path to success. You are also less likely to waste your time trying to do things that you should not spend your time attempting to accomplish.

Additionally, bringing in mentors and advisors can help you expand the size of your team without increasing your costs. People are remarkably willing to lend their expertise, and that frequently includes their operational time and energy. It is more than worth a frank assessment about where your gaps are.

I am not a finance-oriented CEO, so the company brought in a skilled financial controller. The cost was far outweighed by his competency and calmness in doing tasks that had been taking up my time, and more importantly, my brain space. My productivity skyrocketed, and I know now that I should have done that sooner.

Can you accept accountability?

You will have both the privilege of sharing successes with the team you build, and the burden of taking personal responsibility for the actions of that team. A CEO who mentored me calls this "falling on your sword." It falls to you as the founder of the company to take the accountability for failure even if it is not directly "yours." It takes practice to do this with authenticity and believability, but it is absolutely critical.

How tenacious are you?

Can you stick it out even when the wheels seem to be falling off? Or when a naysayer tells you that what you're doing is crazy? And more importantly, can you be tenacious yet remain calm and professional? This takes practice.

Can you find the lessons when things don't go as planned?

Can you pivot and adapt? Because inevitably, things will not go to plan. If you are a person who thrives on order, stability, and control, this may not be the path for you. If you are a person who can create order and stability out of the inevitable chaos, keep reading. It's remarkable how many times your plan, roadmap, or strategy points to "x" outcome and you get off the rollercoaster to find an entirely different landscape. It is not necessarily a bad thing. If you can immediately reassess and determine what to do next without breaking your stride, you can confidently answer yes to this question.

Can you see multiple paths to achieve a goal?

As the founder you will have vision—and most likely, a large personality to deliver on the vision—but many roads lead to Rome. Get your team to Rome with a dose of consensus and logic. The first path may not be the ultimate one. Don't be afraid to get off of it. Don't let ego, cost, fear, or other factors prevent you from exploring or accepting that there are many possible ways to get there.

Can you handle failure and setbacks (without feeling defeated)?

It's important to understand the distinction between defeat and failure. Defeat is the feeling of being demoralized and overcome by adversity after being beaten by something. Failure is simply a lack of immediate success. It is not fatal. It requires refocus and alterations to the strategy to achieve success. If you can quickly refocus and make those adjustments when something has not worked, you understand the distinction. If every failure leaves you feeling defeated and battered, it may be too emotional for you to deal with the constant whiplash and adjustments required to navigate the strategic calibrations you will constantly have to make.

You will also need to be able to differentiate between external and internal factors that contribute to how you handle failure and setbacks. Some external factors are out of your control, like customer sales cycles, management changes, or key team members falling off trucks and breaking bones right at critical customer delivery times. (That last one actually happened to my company!) There are also internal factors, like decisions you've made or intuitions you've trusted that, in hindsight, were not optimal. These will have repercussions, and you have to keep your head up and refuse to feel defeated. Think of the earlier question—can you find the lesson when things don't go as planned; can you pivot and adapt? If you can, you won't feel defeated.

Are you a good listener?

If your answer to this is no—even if the answer to every other question has led you to think that starting a company is the right decision for you—I might advise you to rethink this path. The ability to listen may be the single most important element to success in many ways. You will have to listen to, among a myriad of others: your customers, your team, your mentors, your investors (and the people who choose not to invest), your partners, your vendors, your competition, your family and friends, and your support network. By the end of the day you'll crave silence.

You are not an island. So many of the other questions in this assessment are really hinged on this core competency of being a good listener. Your ability to accept advice and mentorship, collaborate with your team and find multiple paths to a goal, accept support, surface lessons out of failure, pivot and adapt, and fall on your sword only to live another day—these are all skills best executed when you listen keenly. Being an effective and empathetic leader is only possible when you listen deeply to your team, especially when you will likely be asking people to make big sacrifices of their time and take a risk on you.

It is not a dichotomy to be persuasive and tenacious and your company's strongest evangelist while simultaneously being a remarkable listener. In fact, you'll be the most effective at those if you listen carefully. Otherwise you could miss big cues as to what your stakeholders really want and need.

So . . . Are You Ready to Start a Company?

These questions aren't "scored," with a score over a certain number indicating that you should (or shouldn't) decide to start a company. They are designed to make you reflect, with brutal honesty, on whether this path is right for you. These questions are inextricably linked with each other. You need to be articulate in order to be persuasive about why you are embarking on this journey; and you need a strong support system to handle the wild ride.

It is a hard path, but it is rewarding and exhilarating. You will be the architect of your experience, and if that speaks to your personality and to an idea that has been brewing inside of you for a while, give it serious thought. Talk to people who are currently running or who have previously started companies—people with successful exits and people without. Get the real, unvarnished truth about how exciting it is to see your name on patent awards, to speak at conferences, to sit at the head of a conference table, and to see heads nod while you passionately explain your value proposition. Also, get the real, unvarnished truth about the days that aren't so exciting. And then make a decision about whether the idea and the excitement that's burning inside of you is burning so hot that you simply must do this. And if you do decide to take the leap—good luck. And, enjoy.

Notes

"Be Twice as Good"—Yadira Sanchez Olson, "Condoleezza Rice, Olympic medalists look to 'shine a light' on women's empowerment at KPMG summit in Lake County," *Lake County News-Sun*, June 27, 2018.

Sidebar: Marcia Gay Harden—Excerpted from Marc Myers's "Marcia Gay Harden Lost a Bet with Her Mother and Won an Oscar," *Wall Street Journal*, May 1, 2018.

Sidebar: Tory Burch—Excerpted from Clare O'Connor's "Fashion Billionaire Tory Burch Talks Oprah, Eric Schmidt, and the Importance of Thick Skin," *Forbes*, May 9, 2013.

About the Author

Jill Griffin grew up in rural North Carolina surrounded by wonderful teachers who inspired her love of writing. Jill is a Forbes.com contributor, NYSE Independent Director for Luby's/Fuddruckers Restaurants, and an internationally published Harvard Business School "Working Knowledge" author. *Follow These Leaders* is her sixth book.

A huge fan of Austin, Texas, Jill proudly served as Chairwoman for VisitAustin.org for eight years, currently serves on the Executive Committee, and is part of the launch team for VisitAustin Foundation. She also advises ride-share start-up, Hytch, Broadway Bank/Austin, and Central Texas Girl Scouts.

Jill graduated magna cum laude with Bachelor of Science and MBA degrees from the University of South Carolina Moore School of Business, is the recipient of the school's Distinguished Alumna Award, and was the Spring 2018 commencement speaker for MBA and PhD graduates.

Visit jillgriffin.net to discover and connect with Jill Griffin Executive Learning, whose mission is to equip talented people to soar.

INDEX

A

Accountability, accepting, in starting company, 161–162
Achievable, focusing on the, 7
Action
    calling to, xviii
    taking, xix–xx
Adaptation, pivoting and, 162, 164
Adventure, experiencing, 25
Advice
    call to action in, xviii
    common sense in, xviii
    getting from mentors, 32–33, 137
    getting good, 102
    giving good, xxi, 109, 124, 130
    learning curve and, xx
    need for, xx, 161
    paying attention to good, 11
    receptiveness to taking, xix
    seeking of, 148, 150, 151
    soliciting, xvii, 151
    taking, xix, xxi
    worth of, 47–48
Advice giver, bond with advice taker and, xxi
Advice taker, bond with advice giver and, xxi
Advocates, 87, 88, 89
    turning loyal customers into, 92–93
Albrey, Sarah, 48
Albright, Madeleine, 4
Alexander, Dorian, 45–46
Alexander, Justin, 32–33
Alexander, Marsha Griffin, 99–100
Always-on world, 15–16
Amazon.com, 87
Amos, Steve, 29
Angel investors, 56
Angel lenders, 98–103
Articulate, being, in starting company, 159–160
Ask (acquire, specific, know-how, right), 50
Asking for a Friend (Weisberg), xxi
Asking for help, 50
Assumptions, challenging, 44
ASTOUNDZ, 140
Attention, paying, 140
Austin Chamber of Commerce, 49

Authenticity, 74
AutoAlert, LLC, 32
Avery, Christopher, 42–44
AW Media, Inc., 118

B
Banker, relationship with your, 27–28
Barber, Sean, 142–144
Beckham, Odell, Jr., 57
Believability, 107–108
Best intentions, assuming, 60–61
Biblical lessons, applying to life, 124–125
Birkmaier, Bob, 78
Blazers as timeless, 137
Blessings, recognizing your, 133
Borland, 81
Brainstorming with frontline employees, 91
Brand Message Clarity, 12
Brandt, Randy, 150
Bridges, not burning, 75
Brish, Arie, 133
Broadway Bank, 64, 145
Buffett, Warren, 28
Built to Sell (Warrillow), 120
Burch, Tory, 62, 166
Burg, Bob, 73
Bush, George H. W., 4–5
Business, creation of rules for, 119
Busque, Leah, 144
Buy-in, getting, for pitch, 17

C
Cambridge Associates, 155
Canada, Sara, 17–18
CapRidge Partners, LLC, 114

Career advice, 1–83
Career change, making a, 45–46
Carnegie, Dale, 63
Carruthers, Wil, 60–61
Catz, Safra, 72
Champion, finding your, 81
Chapman, Georgina, 148
Clark, Dorie, 56, 77
Cleveland, Mark, 30
Clients, 87, 88, 89
    listening to needs of, 24
    turning repeat customers into, 90–91
Coe, Imogen, 110–111
Cohn, Alisa, 76–77
Colby, Jon, 29
Coleridge, Samuel, xx
Collaboration
    leadership and, 43
    listening and, 62–63
Colotla, Kelly A., 64–65
Comfort zone, moving out of, 22–23
Commitment, 34
Common sense, 104
    in advice, xviii
Communication, effective, 138–139
Company, readiness to start a, 118–125, 155–165
    accepting accountability in, 161–162
    articulation in, 159–160
    being good listener in, 164–165
    conflict management, 160
    emotional toll in, 156–157

financial sacrifice in, 156
finding lessons in adapting, 162
handling failure and setbacks in, 163
loneliness in, 158
multiple paths in achieving goals in, 162–163
need for advice and mentorship, 161
need for immediate gratification, 158–159
persuasiveness in, 159
tenaciousness in, 162
working long hours in, 157–158
Compensation, 74
Compliments, giving, 117
Confidence, turning point for, 22
Conflict management, in starting company, 160
Connections, focusing on, 74
Control, taking, 21
Cooper, Mel, 101–103
Coutee, Miranda, 141
Coutee, Todd, 62–63
Covey, Stephen, 93–94
Creative, being, 7
Crowdsourcing your ideas, 17–18
C-Suites, 68, 152
desire for women in, 8
Customers
loyalty to, 87–94
turning first-time, into repeat, 90–91
turning loyal, into advocates, 92–93
turning qualified prospects into first-time, 90
turning repeat into clients, 88–91
Customer service, 24, 149

D

Damon, Matt, 118
Danos, Patti, 42
Day, recapping your, 53
Decision, changing mind about, 9–11
Defeat, handling in starting company, 163–164
DeNucci, Patti, 121–123
DeNucci & Co. LLC, 121
Difference, making a, 114
Directness, 7
Discouragement, success and, 63
Doughtie, Lynne, 8
Dresselhaus, Mildred S., 18
Dressing for success, 137

E

Echelon Copy, 120
eLearning, 43
Emails, returning, 145
Emotional toll, being prepared for, in starting company, 156–157
Entrepreneur readiness audit, 72
Envy as crippling, 82–83
Epstein, Adam J., 136
Epstein, Ira, 136
EQ (Emotional Quotient), 36
Evans-Martin, Fay, 54–55
Everyone, treatment of, 146
Example, leadership by, 29
Executive coaches, 67–68

Expedia Cruise Ship Centers of Mill Creek, 38

F

Facebook, 155
Failure, 63
    fear of, 42–44
    handling in starting company, 163–164
    success and, 63
Family Dollar, 61
Family lessons, 52–53
The Farmer's Almanac, 151
Fears, facing your, 25
Feloni, Richard, 32, 112
Financial sacrifice, being prepared for, in starting company, 156
Firing, 78
First-degree network, 70
First impressions, 137
First-time customers, 87, 88, 89
    turning into repeat customers, 90–91
Fisher, Eileen, 34
Fitzpatrick, Bill, 124–125
Fitzpatrick, Molly, 39–40
Flanagan, Lauren G., 73–74
Focus, 6
Fresh start, getting a, 19–20
Frost, Robert, 42
Fudge, Melissa, 81
Fuel Capital, 108
Fuller, R. Buckminster., 43

G

Gaddy, Ellen, 1
Gandhi, Mahatma, 119
Gangloff, Joe, 47–48
Gantapanan, Jane Frances C., 138–139
Garvey, Melinda, 118
Genuineness, 147–148
Ghosn, Caroline, 38
Gilbride, Melissa, 24
Girl Scout cookies, selling door-to-door, 49
Gitomer, Jeffrey, xviii
GM Brazil, 23
Goals, multiple paths in starting company, 162–163
The Go-Giver: A Little Story About a Powerful Business Idea (Burg and Mann), 73
Golden Rule, 52
Goldsmith, Marshall, 50
Gorbachev, Mikhail, 4–5
Government, working for, 27
Gratification, need for immediate in starting company, 158–159
Griffin, Jill., 137, 167
Growth, experiencing, 27
Gut, trusting your, 36

H

Hallman, John, 107–108
Hallman Group, 107–108
Handshakes, doing deals on, 101–103
Handwritten notes, sending out, 94
Happiness for another's success, 84–85
Harden, Marcia Gay, 40, 166
Hargett, Karen, 115
Hasson, Ralph, 82–83

Hawthorn, Neal, 80–81
HealthCode, 29
Heart, bringing your big, 109
Helgesen, Sally, 50
Helleher, Herb, 109
Hendricks, Barbara, 119
Herodotus, 124
Hicks, Dan, 19
Highs, managing, 136
HillCo Partners, 66
Hiring, 78
Holder, Julie Fasone, 67–68
Holford, Diana, 21
Holland-Nelson, Leisa, 140
Home, leaving, 129–130
Homelite Textron, 29
Honesty, 127–128
Horn, Chaz, 12
Hotel California, 38
Hours, working long, in starting own company, 157–158
How Women Rise: Break the 12 Habits Holding You Back from Your Next Raise, Promotion, or Job (Helgesen and Goldsmith), 50
Huang, Chieh, 106
Huffington, Arianna, 112
Humility, leadership and, 54–55
Humor in saving steps, 50
Hussein, Sajid, 138
Hytch LLC, 30–31

I

I Am (Kasanoff), 131
Ideas, crowdsourcing your, 17–18
iGen/Gen Z thinkers, 102
Immediate gratification, need for, 158–159
Importance
 recognizing, 99–100
 urgency versus, 106
Inclusivity, 73–74
Influence, 74
inGenious and Creativity Rules (Seelig), 44
Ingenious Designs, 108
Initiative, taking, 21
Instincts, trusting your, 54
Integrity, 127–128
 practicing, 101–103
Interviewing, getting hired and, 64
I Ought to Be in Pictures, 40
Ireland, Kathy, 74

J

James, Kristen, 147–148
Jets.com, 24
JFH Insights, 67
Job interviews, 32
Johnson, Peggy, xix
Jones, Marsha, 66
Jones Lang LaSalle, 21

K

Kasanoff, Bruce, 131–132
Kasper, Ann, 34–35
Keeton, Carole, 114
Keller, Diana, 37
Kerrigan, Nancy, 19–20
Kim, Jim Yong, 55
Knight, Hilary, 37
Knox, Roy and Norma, 58
Korbel, Josef, 4
KPMG Women's Leadership

Summit, xvii, 3, 8, 19, 37

L

Lander, Bob, 15
Lanier, Gayle, 32
Lauder, Estée, 59
Leadership
    collaborative, 43
    by example, 29
    humility and, 54–55
    lack of women in, 72
    in trade association, 94
Leadership Credo, writing, 67–68
The Leadership Gift Program, 43
Learning, 19, 40, 43, 71, 72
    deep, 152
    forever, 57
Learning conferences, attending, 94
Learning curve, advice and, xx
Lee, Brian, 31
Leva, Carey, 145
Levo, 38
Lieblein, Grace, 22–23
Life
    applying biblical lessons to, 124–125
    owning your, 120
Life advice, 97–165
Lincoln, Abraham, 67
Lipinski, Tara, xix
Listening, 6, 150
    collaboration and, 62–63
    importance of, 69
    to the music, 30–31
    with open mind, xix
    in staring own company, 164–165
Liu, Betty, xviii
Loneliness, being prepared for, in starting own company, 158
Looking the part, 116–117
Love, feeling, xxi
Lowe, Cathey, 51
Lows, managing, 136
Loyalty, building, 87–94
    by stages, 88–89
Lucas Point Ventures, 134
Ludy's Fuddruckers Restaurant, 62, 146

M

Management of highs and lows, 136
Mangano, Joy, 108
Mann, John David, 73
Manos, Kris, 12
Marchesa fashion label, 148
Marcus, Stanley, 140
Marketing, importance of, 76–77
Martin, Steve, 29
Mathias, Lee, 36
Maxwell, Earl, 47
Maxwell, John, 116–117
Maxwell, John C., 119
Mayfield, James, 98
McCarty, Daisy, 12
Meanness, 80–81
Medin, Shon, 25–26
Meguschar, David, 73
Men, self-confidence in, 8
Mentor(s), xviii, xix
    age of, 77
    defined, 38

finding, 57
getting advice from, 32–33, 46, 47, 70–72, 82–83, 139
seeking out, 6
Mentoring, 34, 38, 57
importance of, 57
in starting own company, 161
Middle management, 131
Miller, Lucas, 120
Mills, L. C., 117
Mind, changing your, 9–11
Mindset, changing your, 21
Mistakes, admitting to, 9–11
Morgan, Beth, 76
Mullins, Janet Barry, 129–130
Murie, Mardy, 39–40
Music, listening to the, 30–31
Musk, Elon, 66

N

Nabers, Lynn, 75
Nabers, Mary Scott, 75
Nationwide Insurance, 78
Negativity, shrugging off, 66
Negotiation, winning in, 33
Network, building a, 77
Networking, 64–65, 70–72
first-degree, 70
second-degree, 70
Network Kinetix, 70, 153
The New Home Company, 51
New people, openness to, 70–72
Noonan, Tom, 57
No Parking. No Halt. Success Non Stop! (Ratna), 65
Noveck, Beth Simone, 61

O

Olson, Yadira Sanchez, 166
Onboarding, 67
Openness
in listening, xix
to new people, 70–72
Opportunities, looking for new, 64–65
OSMs, 25

P

Parenting, advice about, 20
Parenzan, Carol, 122
Parks, Howard Allen, 121–123
Partnerwerks, Inc., 42
Parton, Dolly, 36
Passion to serve, 141
Penick, Harvey, 150
Pepperidge Farm Bakeries, 146
Performance reviews, 76
Perseverance, 97, 130
Personal work ethic, 10
Perspective, trying new, 115
Persuasiveness in starting company, 159
Phone calls, returning, 145
Pincelli, John, 109
Pinnergy, 80–81
Pivoting, 15
and adaption, 123, 162, 164
Placement, successful, 138–139
Plan
making a, 37–38
for success, 37–38
Portillo, Margo, 27–28
Positive, being, 7
Prager, Jerome L., 124

Preparedness, 32–33
Prospects, 87, 88, 89
    turning qualified, into first-time customers, 90
Punctuality, 7

Q

Questions
    anticipating, 6
    asking, 6, 117, 122, 155, 156
Quinton, Adam, 134–135

R

R. J. Reynolds, 47
Rae, Cheryl, 104-106
Rappoport, Gene, 140
Ratan, Abhishek, 65
Receptiveness to taking advice, xix
Receptivity, 74
Relationships, building, 74
Relationship stages
    advocate, 87, 88, 89, 92–93
    building loyalty in, 88–89
    client, 87, 88, 90–91
    first-time customers, 87, 88
    prospect, 87, 88, 89
    repeat customers, 86, 88, 89, 90–91
    suspect, 87, 89–91
Repeat customers, 87, 88, 89
    turning first-time customers into, 90–91
"Resilience and Grit: The Making of a Champion" (Hicks), 19
Resourcefulness, 12
The Responsibility Process, 43–44

Rice, Condoleezza, 3–5
Richards, Tissa, 70–72, 153
Robertson, Heather, 38
Robinson, Susan, 9–10
Rosewall Press, 121
Rules
    creation of, for business, 119
    one simple, 145
Ryan, Tim, 69

S

St. David's Foundation, 47
St. Vincent Millay, Edna, 11
Salb, Stephanie, 112
Sanford Technology Ventures Program, 43
Saw, taking time to sharpen, 93–94
Schell, Tracy Prager, 124
Schuller, Robert, 42
Scowcroft, Brent, 4
Seasonal workers, 58–59
The Seasons of My Mother: A Memoir of Love, Family, and Flowers (Harden), 40
Second-degree network, 70
Seelig, Tina, 44
Self-confidence in women, 8
Self-discipline, 97
Self-employment, 27
Self-preservation, 97
Semper Fi, 48
Seneca, 100
Serve, passion to, 141
Setbacks, handling in starting company, 163–164
Sharpe, Molly, 104

Shaw, George Bernard, 75
Shelton-Keller Group, 37
Showing up, 34–35
Silhanek, Fred J., 146
Simon, Neil, 40
Simple, keeping, 110-111
Skarphéôinsson, Gylfi, 52–53
Skoggard, Mark, 47–48
Slowing down, 15–16
Smith, Ken, 131
Smith, Ralph, 114
Social capital, cashing in on, 121–123
Soft skills, 60
Southwest Airlines, 109
Spreadfast Software, 81
Stacy, Tom, 80
Stakeholder input, getting, 17–18
Staubach Company, 21
Stevens, Becca, 104
Strategic Partnerships, 75
Stress management, 25
Stretch assignments, taking on, 22–23
Stretching, 8
Success
    dressing for, 137
    planning for, 37–38
Sugarman, Suzanna, 6
Suspect(s), 87, 89
    qualifying, 89–90

T

Tardiness, 48
TaskRabbit, 144
Taylor, Kathy, 127–128
Taylor, Randy, 80–81
Team
    building good, 38
    hiring the best, 7
Teamwork Is An Individual Skill (Avery), 43
TED talks, 77
Tenaciousness in starting company, 162
Theft, 48
Thistle Farms, 104
Thomas, Jeff, 60
Thompson, Carol, 49–51
Thompson, Lexi, 130
3b2 Solutions, 124
Time management, 25, 104–106
TNT, 48
Toastmasters, 65
Trade association, leadership role in, 94
Tramex Travel, 27–28
Treatment of everyone, 146
Trust
    importance of, xix–xx
    in your gut, 36
Truth, need for in advice, xviii
Turnarounds, 138
Turning point, 13–14
Turnover, 48

U

Urgency, versus importance, 106
USI Insurance Services, 73–74

V

Value, 74
    undercutting your, 142–144
Vestage, Margrethe, 80
VF Corp., 47

Visibility, 64–65
VisitAustin.org, 57
VisitCalifornia, 15
VistAustin.org, 15

W

Waiting, 112–113, 150
Walker, Jennifer, 15
Walking away, 115
Walton, Bill, 30
Warner, Mark, 46
Warrillow, John, 120
Washington, George, xxi
Watching, 150
Webb, Lisa, xix–xx
We Bought a Zoo (movie), 118
Weisberg, Jessica, xxi
West, Cornel, philosophy of, 135
West, Vicki Knox, 58–59
Whaley, Suzy, 13–14
Wie, Michelle, 131
Wilson, Hack, 104
Wilson, NeCall, 149
Winfrey, Oprah, 74
Wisdom, 152
    honoring, 76–77
Women
    availability to do anything, 49–51
    capability of, 49–50
    desire for in C-suite, 8
    lack of, in leadership, 72
    self-confidence in, 8
    voicing of opinion by, 48
Women Make Great Leaders, xxi
Work basics, making list of, 6–7
Work ethics, having strong, 10

Working behind the scenes, 134–135
Wrenn, Greg, 81
Wrong, going, 119
Wu, Gillian, 110–111

X

Xylo Technologies, 25–26

Y

Yes, saying, 8–9
Young, Mary, 39
Young Women's Alliance, 50

Z

Zuckerberg, Mark, 155

CPSIA information can be obtained
at www.ICGtesting.com
Printed in the USA
LVHW030807140519
617488LV00001B/1/P